Experiential Therapy for Co-dependency

Experiential Therapy for Co-dependency

by

Sharon Wegscheider Cruse
Joseph R. Cruse
George ("Big Dog") Bougher

Science and Behavior Books, Inc.
Palo Alto, California

Printed in the United States of America.

Library of Congress Number 90-062016

ISBN 8314-0075-7

Cover and interior design by Bird Publishing

Editing by Steve Beitler

Typesetting by BookPrep

Printing by Haddon Craftsmen

Contents

Contents

Contents

Preface

For many years I have been facilitating groups whose goal is to bring hope and healing to individuals, couples and families in pain. My early groups were run in the traditional style of therapy groups, meeting weekly on an out-patient basis.

Later, the techniques of sculpture, psychodrama, and gestalt took me from weekly sharing groups to intensive two- and three-day programs. Finally, an eight-day intensive treatment program was developed.

My style of therapy has moved from traditional "sharing" and "talk" sessions to professionally directed healing sessions. The success of these groups has prompted therapists and counselors to ask me to develop an institute where these methods could be taught.

Our training institute at Onsite has been offered every summer for the past few years; this manual is the text we use. May it bring you creativity, skill, stimulation and clarity as you use its ideas in your groups.

—Sharon Wegscheider Cruse

For more information on the Onsite Institute, please contact Onsite Training & Consulting, 2820 West Main Street, Rapid City, SD 57702; or phone us at 605-341-7432.

A Note About Language

This book uses the personal pronoun "he" for the sake of consistency. Obviously, the ideas presented and experiences recounted are equally relevant to women.

1
Models
and
Philosophy

Sharon Wegscheider Cruse

It's good to be a seeker and a learner, but sooner or later, it's time to take what we have learned and begin to share with anyone who will listen.
—Dag Hammerskjold

> ## There are no experts other than the one you become.

Virginia Satir once paid me a great compliment. She said that I possessed two great gifts. One was that I knew what I didn't know, which kept me open to new ideas. The other was that I was a great creator. The thesaurus describes a creator as one who calls into being, builds, originates, generates, constructs, gives birth to, invents, etc.

Being a creator is the style of therapy I've developed for myself. I hold myself responsible for my actions and I tend to hold others responsible for theirs. This has helped bring out the best in me and in others.

As a creator, I have done best when combining my skills with those of others. The two people who have helped me define and create our models have been my husband, Joe Cruse, and our clinical director, George (Big Dog) Bougher. This chapter will spell out the special philosophy and skills we each bring to our work.

I'm an idea person. The ideas just keep coming to me. As a matter of fact, part of my recovery from workaholism has been to learn to not have to be responsible for every idea I get. I'm now much more selective about which ideas to act on, embellish, forget, or pass on to someone else.

Joe is a scientist. He wants specificity, proof, reasoning, data, etc. His influence on me and our programs has been invaluable. He has brought accountability and credibility to our work.

George is an artist. He uses music, art, story and drama. The three of us synthesize art (feelings), science (thought) and skill (behavior) and are able to develop programs that promote healing.

Education attempts to teach us how to learn from someone else's experience. Our training goal at Onsite is to help each student learn experientially.

> # We look for the master inside each of you.

All therapists need to build a base. To me, to build the base is to become familiar with, and skilled in, many forms of psychotherapy. In *The Psychotherapy Handbook,* Richie Herink described more than 250 therapies in use today. He speaks of Psychoanalysis, Transactional Analysis, Behavior Modification, Gestalt, Psychomotor Therapy, Marriage & Family Therapy, plus 244 more.

As Dr. Albert Schweitzer told Norman Cousins, "We doctors just simply release the little doctor inside the patient." So do we release the natural creative therapist in each of you to do your good work in releasing the patient's own therapist (doctor) inside of him.

Most therapists become involved primarily in their own school of thought and cut themselves off from other areas. Unfortunately, these disciplines themselves often tend to bias the practitioner and thus limit the creativity of that person. Too often, we end up with psychologists, social workers and family and marriage counselors with little versatility and creativity. The result is that the patient (client) must then be "molded" into the treatment mode with which the therapist is most familiar, rather than experiencing a therapy and treatment mode selected because it best fits the patient's particular need.

Each person who plans to become a therapist has the responsibility to learn what is already known. Then the challenge arises. How do I become an effective therapist capable of doing great work? We do so by taking what we have learned and adding our own creativity to it. By adding our special talents and gifts, we create our own therapeutic magic!

It is the genius and courage of a particular person with an active imagination and vision that give birth to a better way of doing something. A good therapist tries an idea, gets results, evaluates the results, refines and polishes and tries it again. After several tries, one comes up with the theory of what worked and why.

> ### All new theories were once "an inspiration."

I'm a creator, a risk-taker and a synthesizer. I have learned that in order to consistently offer quality, whether in treatment, teaching or training, one needs to create a model that can be understood, evaluated, and changed.

The Creation of a Model

For some time, people have asked, "Sharon, how do you work with people? What makes the programs at Onsite so powerfully helpful and healing for people? Why do people register a year ahead just to get into a training institute at Onsite?"

This has forced me to examine and articulate the approach that has been developed in our programs and why it is so useful.

> **Over the years, in training the therapists who work with us, I simply called our approach "experiential therapy."**

As I went through years of training myself, I learned many philosophies, techniques, styles and models. Yet I knew I could never be *only* a Transactional Analysis therapist, a reality therapist, an analyst, a dream therapist, a social worker, a psychologist, a chemical dependency counselor, a psychodramatist or a gestaltist. It would have been too difficult for me to choose.

I needed to use some of each of those methods, philosophies and tools. So I proceeded to learn and train in many disciplines. In some I studied only the basics, some I studied and trained in depth, and in others I pursued degrees. Then, in my own way, I put together a "style."

For many years, I worked successfully with individuals, couples and families. As I watched people recover from past histories and current traumas, I found the work was extremely fulfilling. Many would say I had a "magic" about my work and it could only be done by me. I disagreed with that and felt that many therapists could work with the style I'd created and make "magic" in their own ways.

I proceeded to invite therapists to our center and our home, and over the years, a style that can be described, understood, taught and evaluated has evolved. Meanwhile, thousands of patients, clients, and participants have been involved.

My first programs were developed in the early '70s; now, some 20 years later, we have a solid methodology. Part of the "magic" is that the methodology is a framework that allows for an ongoing creative process. From Fritz Perls:

> A thousand plastic flowers
> Don't make a desert bloom
> A thousand empty faces
> Don't fill an empty room

I'm not interested in a fixed, static model of working. It's important to me to provide a flexible framework with concrete suggestions for adding creativity to your work. My goal is to use specific therapeutic methods that allow patients to move beyond thoughts, feelings and behaviors that are self-defeating, in order to heal and offer choices.

Experiential therapy works with the "whole" person. It's therapy that is based on reality. Years ago, Fritz Perls said:

"Health is an appropriate balance of the coordination of all of what we are."

In therapy we must address our whole selves. This means the therapy approach must recognize and heal the:

- thinking (cognitive) part of ourselves
- feeling (emotional) part of ourselves

- acting (behavioral) part of ourselves
- meaning (spiritual) part of ourselves

Secondly, we as whole people (organisms) must exist in a context. We live in relationship to others. Some of those relationships include families (past and present), sometimes they involve a primary partner. Then there are friends, employers, etc.

Just based on the above, it is becoming clear that the full healing of a person requires therapy that is cognitive, emotional, behavioral, and spiritual. Such therapy addresses both the self and significant relationships.

In my work, this means I need to have a wide range of skills to be most helpful to the people I work with.

> ## Some of my most valuable lessons have been rather simple lessons learned from wise and profound people.

FROM FRITZ PERLS

I learned that it is important for each client to carefully recapture and re-own the discarded and disowned parts of the self. As this recapturing occurs, the person becomes strong enough to continue growth on his own. A therapist has done a good job when he or she is no longer needed and the person becomes his own therapist.

FROM BARRY STEVENS

I learned to *"Use whatever is at hand."* People are constantly giving messages to the therapist or the group. There are tones, voice inflections and verbal clues to feelings, such as body language, tears, etc. Everything meaningful is happening in the present. In a workshop I attended by John Stevens, Barry Stevens' son, he said, *"Lose your mind, and come to your senses."*

> ## The skilled and attentive therapist is fully present and sensually alive.

We are closer to health when we take responsibility for our every emotion, movement, and thought—and shed responsibility for the emotions, movements, and thoughts of others.

9

FROM VIRGINIA SATIR

Beyond the goal of healing the self and reaching one's full potential as a person, Virginia's gift to the world included integrating the need to grow healthy in relationships, sometimes with another person and sometimes within a system.

> ## She taught me to attempt to heal current pains, reawaken old dreams and wishes, and give myself permission to develop new dreams.

FROM NORMAN COUSINS

I learned that personal responsibility must be taken by all people who want to become more fully healthy. Whether the person is recovering from physical disease or spiritual/emotional disability, much will depend on a person's willingness to take responsible action.

> ## Cousins has taught us that the mental states and attitudes of patients have a lot to do with the course of their diseases.

He states that the body's defense against infection depends in large part on the mechanisms of immunity and that these mechanisms are influenced by our mental states.

Emotional states have long been known to affect the secretion of certain chemicals. The brain contains substances that are chemically related and go by the name "neurotransmitters." The interplay between mind-body-emotions is an important link in healing.

FROM NATHANIAL BRANDEN

> ## This core issue was the loss of self-esteem.

I learned that regardless of the particular problem for which a client or patient sought help, there was basically one core issue that manifested itself in each person.

FROM SHELDON KOPP

I learned that the therapist is an observer and a catalyst, and is there to assist the client on his personal spiritual journey.

> **Each client is on his own pilgrimage and the therapist is at best a guide.**

In his book, *If You Meet the Buddha on the Road, Kill Him,* Kopp says,

> *"You can stay at home, safe in the familiar illusion of certainty. Do not set out without realizing that the way is not without danger. Everything good is costly and the development of the personality is one of the most costly of all things. It will cost you your innocence, your illusions, your certainty."*

FROM W. HUGH MISSILDINE, MD

I learned that much distress, fatigue, loneliness, hurt, shame, guilt and inner emptiness could be eliminated if people had a deeper understanding of and love for their "inner child."

We all have an "inner child of the past" that affects what we feel and do.

> **This inner child can either be a wounded part of ourselves that keeps us in a self-defeating lifestyle, or it can become our guide and mentor.**

Making peace with this inner child of the past is essential to therapy.

There are many more who have added to my ideas, thoughts, and skills as a therapist. My colleague, George ("Big Dog") Bougher, tells his patients about a man who attempted to teach him how to sculpt. Big Dog was excited about sculpting a beautiful piece, and yet when his teacher began giving his instructions, he had George build a base first. "You can't build sculpture without a base." This was a boring disappointment.

For some time Big Dog shaped, reshaped and worked on the base, never quite getting his teacher's approval. Finally one day he went to his teacher, fully bored and tired of trying to get it perfect, and said, "It's perfect enough." The teacher said, "So it is," and Big Dog began sculpting. *He had built his base.*

My journey was similar. I studied with many great people, took many courses and lessons, and watched my mentors. Then one day I read these words from Dag Hammerskjold:

> *It's good to be a seeker and a learner,*
> *but sooner or later, it's time to*
> *take what we have learned and begin to*
> *share with anyone who will listen.*

I realized I had built my base.

I knew from that time on that:

1. *I was filled with gratitude.* All of us today in the field stand taller because we stand on the shoulders of those who have gone before us. It was time for me to carry the responsibility, to continue to make my contribution, add to my field and offer my shoulders for others to stand on.

2. *It was time to share my ideas.* I also learned that there are two reasons to make changes and choices. One is to seek change because of pain that is no longer tolerable, and the other is to seek change in order to become more fully human.

> ## *Both therapists and clients must remember that to heal and grow, there are two processes that must be accomplished. One is "learning" and the other is "unlearning."*

The negative rules and excess emotional baggage that many have carried since childhood must be relived, refelt and reunderstood. This is an important part of the therapeutic process. However, many therapists get stuck in this negativity and never get on with the "learning." It is the therapist's job to help the client find new ways of doing things and new ways of coping.

As we work with the clients and patients who come to our programs in the Black Hills, we have goals in mind for each person's work. These goals include:

1. Presenting information that will allow the person to reframe his current thinking and see a bigger picture of reality

2. Reawakening and reordering the emotional and passionate attributes of the individual

3. Breaking the bonds of compulsive behaviors to provide freedom of choice

4. Returning that person to the precious worthwhile self he was before he became traumatized

5. Helping the person develop safe and useful relationship skills

To reach these goals, I needed to develop an eclectic method of addressing the thinking, feeling and behavioral needs of the client.

> ## The method needed to be felt, not just understood.

I also knew instinctively that there needed to be a spiritual component to the healing process. Out of this need came my experiential therapy and my style of using what is at hand and what works. The method blends science, art, and traditional therapy models.

To understand why experiential therapy is so important, it's essential to understand co-dependency. Later on in this book, we will examine the nature of co-dependency. First, we'll hear from an artist-therapist on how art became an integral part of our experiential treatment plan.

George Bougher is known as the "therapist with many colors in his paint box." What this means is that he uses whatever is at hand to make a point that is important and powerful to the patient. George has all the "book and degree" skills a master therapist needs. His brilliance lies in his ability to add music, drama, art and sculpture to access what the client needs to address. This is the "artist" at work.

"Psycho" comes from the Greek goddess Psyche. It personifies the soul. The root of "therapy" is Greek and means taking care of or tending. The meaning therefore of the word psychotherapy is the care and tending of the soul.

There is no doubt in my mind that the healing that comes in therapy comes from a spiritual place. I know it is a risky, and to some an unprofessional, statement to make, but I believe the following to be true.

True therapists are teachers, mentors and demonstrators. Role modeling is a powerful teacher. Each person who becomes a teacher/mentor/counselor brings important ingredients to the work. There is gentleness, a sense of surrender, tolerance, trust, compassion, honesty, joy, patience and a developed *sense* of human integrity.

One of the most important attributes of a healing therapist is the experience of having walked a personal path of recovery. Such a person demonstrates a life-style that the patient/client can learn from.

Most people who seek help are not bad or sick. They are wounded and hurting. They do not need to be badgered or humiliated. They need to be healed and touched. Their diseases may need confrontation (confront their behavior), but their souls (their essences) need healing.

We must carefully nourish their wounded inner selves so they are able to change their self-defeating behavior. Inner healing, not just outward behavior, is what psychotherapy is all about.

Therapists need to be healers, but when healing takes place, it often looks like "magic." Yet it can be explained.

A magical artist of skill and compassion is George ("Big Dog") Bougher. I'm proud to introduce his work in this book.

George ("Big Dog") Bougher

I believe personal recovery and a personal approach to therapy to be the ultimate art form. No longer is art and creativity field-specific (e.g., painting, dance, or poetry). There is also the creativity that is closing the gap between what we know and what, as human beings, we are.

In an age where quantity often overshadows quality, creative living makes it possible to work through issues (as opposed to work on them). It celebrates choice and is centered in wholeness and cohesion.

> ### *Webster's Dictionary defines creative as having the quality of something created rather than 'imitated'.*

I believe that if one never discovers his own goodness and worth, his life will be uncreative, one of mere imitation. People come to therapy because they desire a better quality of life.

In my case I was field-specific as an artist first. I studied painting and sculpture at what is now Carnegie-Mellon University in Pittsburgh,

Pennsylvania. The learning experiences were wonderful as my understanding and appreciation of art, my skills and eye were sharpened. At this time, however, art was the only polished edge of my life. I did not know how to live; I was simply "doing time." Becoming creative with life came later and was a product of my own twelve-step program and co-dependency treatment.

In 1977 I received my Master's degree in counseling from the University of Pittsburgh (another rich experience) and the significance of being an "artist" expanded for me. Using my background as an artist has increased my effectiveness as a therapist.

Today I consider myself an artist-therapist.

> **These two fields have nourished each other over the years, from which I draw this conclusion: being creative in a part of life or in the whole of life requires the willingness to be additive and deductive.**

All else follows.

> *The artist appeals to the part of our being which is not dependent on wisdom.*
> —Joseph Conrad

Picture the sculptor in a studio, working on a clay model. The hands are stained red as clay is slowly added until a full three-dimensional form is shaped. This describes the additive process.

Now picture the same sculptor carving a block of marble. Tools are required to take chips away a little at a time until the result is achieved. This is the deductive process.

Every human being houses such an artist. These additive and deductive processes are innate, totally natural and inside each and every one of us. Both processes are necessary for creative living. The goal of therapy is to access the artist.

The hardest thing to do is start.
—Joe Goto

As a child, one's creativity and self-definition are actively molded by the parents' responses. In the dysfunctional family such children become "adult children" and often cannot create for themselves in a healthy, nurturing style. For them life is a process of duplication, as they can only reproduce what was familiar to them as children. There is very little "original" here—no sense of self. I refer to this style as that of the "craftsman" and not that of an artist. A craftsman only produces more of the same.

One thing I would like to see is parents and educators teaching their children how *to think not* what *to think.*
—Dr. Peter Alsop

This "more of the same" that is manufactured by untreated co-dependents multiplies the burden they've always carried. This burden is their repression, an "emotional abscess" that needs lancing. The pattern continues until one day they can no longer carry it, but they don't know how to get rid of it either. Chemical and/or behavioral compulsions are often welded to this "death style" as constant efforts are needed "to keep the lid" on their boiling cauldron of pain. In short they have become victims of an "additive-only process."

The inevitable events and complications of disabling self-worth, relationships and body follow. The disease of co-dependency is winning, and nothing changes unless this historical repression is removed. Treatment is the beginning of the deductive process. Twelve-step support and follow-up therapy continue to deduct residue until the individual becomes like the tide going in and out; the volume remains the same but the form changes on a daily basis.

> # Treatment is about separating yourself from the disease; you are not the disease!

We have a saying at Onsite: *"Healthy people feel twice and unhealthy people feel once."* This means it is healthy to feel a feeling and then express it. In unhealthy relationships, a person feels a feeling and then—not feeling emotionally safe or welcome to show it—he stuffs the feeling, denies it and represses it. In short, healthy people feel and express; unhealthy people feel and repress. A large share of co-dependency treatment is the exploring and re-feeling of historically repressed emotions, which are stored like a compressed spring. Anger and rage are some of the powerful and volatile emotions that need to be expressed.

Our clients have a communication style that either avoids anger or uses it "sideways," never facing and focusing on its source. In group therapy, the appropriate pacing is different for each client, and it is very important for the therapist to have several anger-release and rage-reduction methods so he can best serve his client. Here are some that I use:

> touching hands firmly (patty-cake style)
> clenching fists
> pushing against a wall, floor or pillow
> pulling a rope or sheet
> twisting a towel into knots
> tearing newspaper
> standing still and yelling (head high and eyes open)
> rolling a towel into a tight long tube and then using it like a bat
> kicking pillows
> throwing a tantrum on a bed of pillows (flailing arms and legs)
> exaggerating a song or poem or vowel sound
> growling like an animal
> pointing and yelling
> whispering
> making a hissing sound
> acting the anger out non verbally (like a dance)
> repeating a significant phrase
> running or stomping in place
> clenching and releasing exercise hand grips
> drawing on paper
> using the Bataka bat on a pillow

All the above help bring the anger/rage up, keep it focused, and involve the entire person (animating and integrating the inside and the outside) in the process.

At least two benefits occur after the discharge of stored feelings. First there is relief and then there is celebration, for the person now knows he can survive his feelings.

"Our feelings won't kill us unless we keep them inside."
—Skip Sauvain

I call this re-feeling and experiencing current feelings *making peace with all the colors in your paint box.* The paint box represents our feelings and full potential. It is all there: standard-issue red, orange, yellow, green, blue, purple, brown and black. There are no good or bad colors and there are no good or bad feelings—they are just real. People in pain often don't know this.

Creative living is being yourself by honoring all your parts and being flexible in making choices (additive and deductive). Creative living brings meaning, form, direction, and purpose to our lives.

> **Becoming a "multi-colored person" and having a rainbow life is our birthright.**

An effective therapist uses all the colors in his paint box. Without the artist-self, therapy will be flat imitation and limited at best. Technique will be used to "rubber-stamp" therapy. Allowing the process to have a life of its own is the way of the artist, and having a "blueprint" approach is the way of the craftsman. A craftsman only has science but a scientist can be an artist!

The disease is the same but the people are different.
—Dr. Joe Cruse

Scientists and artists traditionally have been at loggerheads with each other. Science determines certain perceptions of our reality and art brings meaning to that reality. We need both not only woven into our society but personally integrated as well. I view the "adult" part of a person as the cognitive or scientist part, and the "inner child" as the emotive or artist part of a person. A total scientist has no "heart knowledge" and will be robotic in relationships. On the other hand, the artist without the scientist part operates without structure and boundaries and will suffer from great inspirations that never materialize. Self-synthesis is required.

In summary, if there is no artist there is no art. If there is no art then there is no meaning. If there is no meaning, it's because there is no love.

If there is no love, then there is no spiritual life. If there is no spiritual life, then there is death.

> # The complications of untreated co-dependency give us two kinds of death, the physical death and the "zombie walking" inner death.

I had a great-grandparent who was Native American. Part of my recovery was to claim this historical piece of myself, and during that process I was re-named "Big Dog." This name, like so much of my recovery, has expanded in meaning. It started out being a playful gift, an outpouring of affection, and now it has become my spiritual name.

A member of the Lakota tribe, here in the Black Hills, once told me when the Native Americans of the Great Plains first saw horses, they thought they were big dogs. I was told that "shunka tonka" is Lakota for "big dog."

My spiritual name expanded and has now become an equation for how I describe the role of a therapist. A therapist is a vehicle to guide clients to more prosperity and abundance, just like the horse was to the Native Americans of the Great Plains. I also believe that the client becomes a "big dog" for himself as he begins to parent himself with creative living and a personalized recovery base.

> She had horses who whispered in the dark who were afraid to speak.
> She had horses who screamed out of fear of the silence, who carried
> knives to protect themselves from ghosts.
> She had horses who waited for destruction.
> She had horses who waited for resurrection.
> She had some horses.
> —Joy Hargo, from the poem and book *She Had Some Horses*
>   (Thunder Mouth Press)

Once when I was meditating a suggestion came to me. The suggestion was, "You have been lost in a library, looking for a book that you have written but never read." We each have a book, and my wish for professionals entering the area of experiential therapy is that they find and read their books and use them as a way to display their art before they attempt to become the art teacher.

The following list of attributes makes a healthy therapist:

> has a sense of humor (not sarcasm)
> has knowledge of addiction and co-dependency
> keeps client material confidential
> has individual and group counseling skills
> can confront denial in a fair but firm manner
> maintains boundaries with clients (on and off the job)
> has a sense of responsibility
> has personal integrity and professional ethics
> can tolerate a great deal of complexity and inconsistency
> recognizes own limits and can make appropriate referrals
> does not have his identity tied up with his authority, job or title
> can be objective on the job
> is open to creative criticism
> shows the ability to play
> has social skills and can be a team player
> can share personal experience, strength and hope
> has the ability and willingness to make self-assessments personally
>   and professionally
> understands that his way of facilitating therapy is not the only way
> can survive his own and clients' feelings
> is committed to his own healing and continued healing
> is free or in recovery from all medicators
> understands his own personality style
> has the ability to "catch himself"
> respects the twelve-step support systems

To paraphrase two ancient medical dicta:

> *"Heal Thyself"* and *"Do No Harm."*

> *Experiential therapy takes us beyond what we know.*
> —Big Dog

An art critic once wrote an article about the deep significance of a red sky in a painting by Picasso. One day the writer had the opportunity to meet the great master and was eager to see if his intellectualization matched the painter's intent. Picasso smiled and replied, "I used red because I ran out of blue."

The therapist as an artist must appreciate that the unexpected is to be expected. The first thing Sharon Wegscheider Cruse taught me was the importance of calling "time out" and knowing when to "shift." A prerequisite to developing one's artist part is to accept that in life there is no such thing as a straight line! Oh, there is a geometry of sorts with patterns, tangents, etc.—in fact I call this organic geometry because it is humanized.

I do not work with a client until I have the appropriate data (here again, another base) to build the work in an additive and deductive manner. I then begin "sketching" the client's whole experience—looking for the organic geometry and developing sculpture ideas, knowing that once the work begins the piece may "shift" or be abandoned completely.

Therapists can be preachers or teachers. The preacher is preoccupied with telling someone what to do, but the teacher simply motivates. I believe the highest compliment one can receive is that he is a great teacher.

Part II of this book features 100 sculpture ideas developed at Onsite over the past two years. Joe Cruse developed the system of TUMSS—which specifies each exercise's title, uses, method, and what it simulates, stimulates or both—so their essence and intent can be captured, studied and shared. Some of these sculptures are featured at training institute classes, where the students and group leaders brainstorm, play "what if," dismantle and add until eventually the student personalizes the piece by tapping his own creative process.

The sculptures in Part II are presented for your study and enjoyment. They are meant to have a life of their own as they are not cast in bronze. We hope that they serve to motivate and inspire you and your clients to use more of the colors in the paint box. We are at least artists and at best potentially great masters in our own right. No two artists are alike, and there is nothing that can't be sculpted! Most of the sculptures in Part II were developed by George Bougher.

For twenty years, people have told me that my therapeutic work was magical. Some of them have said that while it was profound in its results, it could probably never be fully understood or taught to others.

Yet, deep down, I knew it could be both understood and taught. There was no doubt in my mind that people in pain were suffering from "a disease."

Working with Joe Cruse has elevated my work with families to a new under-standing. His knowledge of the workings of the brain, addictive disease, dependency, medicine and anthropology blends with the best I've been exposed to in family systems, group dynamics and spirituality.

It is with love and gratitude that I welcome Joe Cruse's contribution to this book.

HEALING

one part science
one part skill
one part compassion
one part recovery
one part spirit
one part knowledge
one part humor
one part mystery
} MAGICAL THERAPY

Because we are addressing a disease that entails significant brain involvement, we need to understand the workings of our brains and the interplay of brain activity and behavior. The scientific contributions of Joe Cruse have helped both our staff and patients to understand and treat co-dependency.

Joseph R. Cruse, M.D.

From an article in *The Journal Of The American Medical Association*
(August 4, 1989, Vol. 262, No. 5) I quote:

> *Peace through mind/brain science was the theme of two conferences held
> in Hamamatsu City, Japan. Discussion at these conferences emphasized
> new imaging technologies, including positive emission tomography
> (PET), that make it possible for the first time* to relate human thought,
> emotions, and behavior to measureable chemical reactions within
> the living human brain.
>
> *At the conclusion of the second conference, the scientists and engineers
> who attended declared their intention to promote the scientific study of
> brain mechanisms involved in destructive and violent behavior, as well
> as those related to loving and creative behavior.*
>
> *The hypothesis is that peace through mind/brain science may be an idea
> whose time has come.*
>
> [Emphasis added]

Ashleigh Brilliant spoke of the body and the brain in the beginning of
his book, *I Have Abandoned My Search for the Truth.* He goes on to say:

The body has strange ways of feeding, eliminating and reproducing that are quite grotesque. Most of these odd characteristics are apparently traceable to earlier times and conditions which our bodies have not yet learned no longer prevail. Learning which does take place occurs in a dense, and rather unlovely organ called the brain. Somehow, it seems there is more of us in our brain than there is anywhere else in our body. In some mysterious way, thinking is the same as being.

[Emphasis added]

Brilliant is saying that things about our bodies and behaviors aren't very different from much earlier times, even in these modern days of increased technology. He implies that these processes should have become more sophisticated in several million years.

This is not unlike the co-dependent who brings childhood (primitive) behaviors, thoughts, and feelings into an adult world of higher functioning and sophistication.

Scientific Basis Of The Disease

THE BRAIN: TARGET ORGAN

We are dealing with the brain when we treat co-dependency. The brain is the primary target organ of both chemical dependency and co-dependency, and indeed many other disorders that previously have been called "mental" illnesses. Actually the term mental illness is a misnomer if we are (from this point forward) going to consider:

1. The brain is a functioning organ with disorders. (measurable)

2. The mind is the seat of complex processes that give evidence of the functioning of that organ. (measurable)

This paradigm, or model, opens up entirely new vistas in psychology and psychiatry (perhaps more accurately described as cerebrology or cerebriatry).

New Science

Mark Gold, M.D., co-founder of the Cocaine Hotline, states now that

Psychiatry is finally out of the mind and into the brain.

Melvin Sabshin, M.D., President and Chairman of the Board of Psychiatric Press, Inc., states in the *APA Textbook of Psychiatry* that

> *Psychiatry is in one of the most exciting, creative, and productive phases of its long history. By the rapid acquisition of new scientific knowledge and catalyzed by external pressures requiring empirically documented objectification, the field is undergoing a significant transformation.*

Dr. Joseph T. Quail of The Johns Hopkins School of Medicine states that

> *With advances in research on the brain over the last* fifteen years *we have now reached the point that neuroscience can justifiably be considered the* biomedical foundation *for psychiatry. Logarithmic growth in our understanding of the organization and functioning of the brain has made it feasible to begin to anlayze behavior at the molecular level.*
>
> [Emphasis added]

These were not popular ideas even fifteen years ago. Tension has developed between:

1. Those defending the old paradigm that the brain is an electrically driven machine whose processes we will never be able to capture and measure exactly, and

2. Those who find themselves on a new shoreline, advocating a view that the brain is a hormonally and chemically modulated gland producing powerful mind-, mood-, and behavior-altering hormones and neurotransmitters.

Advocates of this new paradigm find that confirming research data are pouring out daily and have been for some time. Some clinicians and some programs are now using that data in patient care. We are at Onsite.

This new science has many different names, including neuropsychology, psychoneurobiology and neurochemistry. Jon Franklin, Pulitzer Prize–winning science editor of the *Baltimore Evening Sun,* calls this new science "molecular psychology." Chemicals are made up of molecules, and brain functions now appear to be chemically determined. Franklin uses this description:

The basis of this new discipline is the perception that human thought, emotion, and behavior result from the inner play of molecules across the surface of brain cells. The corollary from which this science grows is that mental processes are therefore quantifiable in chemical terms.

Thomas Kuhn describes the term paradigm in his book, *The Structure of Scientific Revolutions*, as follows:

Without commitment to a paradigm, there can be no science. . . The study of paradigms is what prepares a student for membership in a particular scientific community. Persons whose research and therapy are based on shared paradigms are committed to the same rules and standards of scientific practice.

In designing a treatment program for co-dependency, it is necessary to have a paradigm that provides measurable specificity.

Richard Bergland, M.D. (New York University Medical Center), feels that paradigm is probably the best term for models of thought about the brain and its disorders. He believes that

The existing paradigm that we have used for years about the brain regarding behavior, emotions and thought has ceased to function adequately and . . . we are on the shoreline of a whole new way of thinking of and perceiving the brain and its function.

What is known of this new paradigm is adaptable to the concept of co-dependency. In years to come, researchers will establish links between hormones and other chemicals of the brain and human behavior. This is a tremendous undertaking, but it is now within the realm of possibility. We will then know just how experiential therapy and other cerebro-therapeutic techniques actually affect the function, chemistry and anatomy of our brains. Perhaps then the concept of world peace through imaging and meditation will become a reality.

> **The implication that experiential therapy and re-experiencing emotions can actually change the function and structure of the brain can be overwhelming, but it is indeed possible.**

Jon Franklin succinctly lays out the potential of our brain's ability to change in his book, *Molecules of the Mind.* He states:

> *There are by some estimates, perhaps as many as a trillion cells in the brain. Each one changes status and activity by the moment, exquisitely sensitive to the outside environment, storing, processing, changing, ever changing, ever embedded in the rich chatter of chemical messages that alter their meanings and context in accordance with complex behaviors, transformations and feedback loops. At any instant, a cell's variables offer choices more numerous than the total number of all the elemental particles in the entire universe! The result of this interplay is the multiplex structure of human thought and emotions (and behavior and spiritual connection) that we refer to as personality.*

Structure, function and behavior all affect one another. Actual structural changes in the connections between neurons and the workings of certain centers in our brain can occur. Sometimes, the workings shut down and become atrophied because of disease, or flare up and become dominant because of overuse. At other times, the brain can change its functioning entirely because of new needs and new stimuli. We constantly adapt and change circuitry in our brains as we continue to cope with our environment. Other times we are "stuck" with our systems as they are and need an intervention to jog us free. We need to have our brains stimulated.

One of the most effective ways to provide this stimulation is to direct the patient to establish and experience certain stimuli, thereby bringing forth renewed energy and renewed commitment to becoming unstuck. This is the purpose of the experiential therapy: to re-experience thoughts, behaviors, and emotions and deal with them in order to heal them and be done with them. Other thoughts, feelings and behaviors may not heal as well and will need to be modified to cause us less pain. Finally, some thoughts, feelings and behaviors can actually become (through understanding) "helpers" to us as we encounter new circumstances.

With proper therapy for this disease, our lives become much more manageable.

Therapeutic techniques and the therapist must be versatile. Thoughts, feelings and behaviors change the brain in a number of surprising ways. We previously thought the brain was essentially unchangeable, and "what you have is all you get." Research shows that neurons, binding sites, control centers and entire brain systems can be changed. (Ashton, 1987).

Repetitive thinking, feeling and behaving can change many of the working *systems* of the brain. If a brain is constantly stimulated by anxiety-producing thoughts, emotions and actions, eventually the brain systems change to produce anxiety in response even to "slight" stimuli that to most people would not be anxiety-producing.

In addition, repetitive thoughts, feelings and actions cause actual gain or loss in the number and size of certain brain cells and can change the number and kinds of connections among our brain cells; thus the *anatomy* is changed. Likewise, other ways of changing the *anatomy* of the brain (surgery, trauma, tumors) can certainly change the working *systems* of the brain as well as an individual's *thoughts, feelings* and *behaviors.*

For many years, an uneasy tension often arose between medical science and the spiritual disciplines. Programs such as Alcoholics Anonymous have helped reduce that tension and bridge these two fields by incorporating the insights of both. Our growing understanding of co-dependency is strengthening that bridge. This leads us now to examine the spiritual dimension of co-dependency.

Spiritual Dimension

Some fear that a "chemical" perspective on co-dependency and addiction will replace a "spiritual" perspective. That is an unnecessary fear, as the dimensions of human disease include behavioral, intellectual, emotional and spiritual aspects; the entire human condition cannot be encompassed *only* chemically. Yet, we are less than fully knowledgeable therapists or healers if we ignore any one aspect.

> *The next century is going to see a dramatic process of discovery in which molecular defects are connected one after another to mental illnesses and mental disorders. It's difficult, looking at what's on our plate, not to be dumbfounded, and paralyzed by the possibilities.*

Disease Model vs. Adaptive Model

The *disease model* of co-dependency is being challenged by the adaptive model—the idea that co-dependency is simply a problem of maladaptation to stress or life events. Centuries ago, all diseases were considered maladaptive in that they were thought to result from the individual's maladative behavior, morals, thoughts and beliefs.

A disease model is attractive because it works. It helps us maintain specificity as we work with the patient and with fellow professionals. The adaptive model does not withstand scientific scrutiny or actual quantification as to what it is we are doing or have done. The adaptive model is intuitively appealing to the mind because it is based on centuries-old philosophical superstition and religious incantations. But the Adaptive Model can cause us to actually go backwards and impede the therapeutic process.

Chemical theories about the brain are not entirely new. There were hints as far back as the 1800s that certain chemicals were capable of altering the heart rate in animals, and that the brain actually changed its chemical makeup when behavior changes were forced upon it. Some readers may feel a sense of resistance or discomfort with the concept of mental illness as a chemical brain disorder, an idea that puts thought and mental disorders second.

If this was known in the '60s and '70s, no one really had the interest or enough information to put such knowledge to good practical use. Psychologists and others in the '50s, '60s and '70s were focused almost universally on the environment and the behavior of the individual. Behavior and environment are just two aspects of co-dependency or any other illness, as we will demonstrate later when we talk about the person, the process and environment.

Those of you who were trained in the '60s and '70s are familiar with the conflict that exists between the scientific community and the adapative or humanistic community.

The division between these approaches in our country can be likened to the centuries-old differences between Eastern and Western medicine. Those in the West direct their therapeutic efforts toward precise correlations as to cause and effect, dealing in signs and symptoms, setting minimum criteria for diagnosis and expecting continual re-evaluation. Those dealing in Western medicine expect to see measureable levels of recovery following an intervention and certain treatment plans.

In the East, however, healers go forward knowing that new knowledge of the ebb and flow of chemicals within the body supports much of what they have taught for centuries. They have always known that healing, religion, meditation and prayer needs emanate from the same source.

Recently, the mainstream of scientific concern in this country and twelve-step programs have begun to converge. Spiritual searches now resemble scientific inquiries.

> # The nature-vs.-nurture controversy is becoming the nature-plus-nurture dynamic.

In an effort to avoid the cold and unsatisfying equations of mathematician, physicist, or chemist, Jon Franklin states that the mind/brain's functioning is a product of its ever-changing ingredients.

It is a dollop of heredity, mixed well with a mother's smile, blended with a virus or two, and leavened with a kick in the tail, two jiggers of brandy, and a lottery ticket just one number off the money.

Another important aspect of the emerging medical model is that it relies heavily on the individual's responsibility for himself. The recovery from the illness is up to the patient, whereas in the adaptive model the client has been consumed by outside forces that conspired to undermine his maturity, ability to cope, or ability to recover.

Convergence

It is obvious that the work of various authors on co-dependency is beginning to converge. The rigid boundaries between medical, scientific, social, spiritual, mental-health, and psychological disciplines are beginning to soften.

It is well stated by Norman Cousins how holistic health and other deviations from the medical mainstream have been compelling, productive and yet non-specific enough to result in confusion and division. Para-psychology and a flood of new-age philosophies and practices have chosen bits from both Eastern and Western practices and beliefs.

Many of these approaches claim that "this is the way, the *only* way." However, many such techniques have a basis in fact, have validity, and can be effective. It is their exclusive, inappropriate and exaggerated use that results in unfavorable outcomes.

Other theories contradict one another and have no basis in fact. They are thrust upon a needy public. Some samples of what's available are:

      astrology
      graphology
      numerology
      clairvoyance
      homeopathy
      naturopathy
      nutrient science
      psychic surgery
      faith healing
      vitamin therapy
      apricot kernel therapy
      touch encounters
      negative ionization
      crystal therapy
      psychocalisthenics

More troublesome are the schools of:

      prememory breathwork
      regression therapy
      rebirthing

At different times, the latter methods utilize metabolic-, mind- and mood-altering techniques of hyperventilation, forced expiration, (valsalva maneuver), hypnosuggestion, chemical sedation and regression. This is harking back to the '60s and the drug-using mind-expansion communities.

Perhaps parapsychological techniques can be safe and effective in the hands of the originators, but they can be quite dangerous and damaging in the hands of those who might hang out a shingle after attending a workshop or one training course on the use of the technique.

The brain is so programmable that *belief* in cutting the left index fingernail on the third Tuesday of each month may actually result in diminishing certain ailments—for a time. The effect is real, but the process is based more on the brain's own self-healing through belief rather than any external technique, even though the technique serves as a catalyst. Also because of the placebo phenomenon, such techniques appear useful and valid.

Cousins is an "arbitrator" between the holistic health community and medicine as it was in the '60s and '70s. The manner in which he lays out the arguments for many perspectives in his book, *Anatomy of An Illness,* is non-controversial, supportive and quietly authoritative to both sides.

Having had an opportunity to spend an afternoon with Cousins and accompany him through the Eisenhower Medical Center, an advanced medical institution 90 miles southeast of Los Angeles, I was taken with his conviction and clarity. Here is what he states in his book:

> While it is reasonable to expect the physician to take the concept of holistic health seriously, it is unreasonable to expect him or her to embrace approaches which lack systematic and sustained verifiable data. Similarly, it is reasonable to expect physicians to maintain open minds about new developments in diagnosis and treatment, even though they may not seem to be in harmony with their own training and experience.

> It is not reasonable to expect a physician to proceed with treatments in the absence of adequate clinical evidence that the treatment is safe and efficacious. No responsible physician will experiment with patients. It is reasonable to expect a physician to recognize that science does not have all the answers yet to problems of health, healing (and, especially, I might add, of spirituality). But it is not reasonable to expect physicians to give up their scientific method in treating patients.

We concur that the most important thing about science is the scientific method—a way of thinking systematically, a way of assembling evidence and appraising it, and a way of conducting our business so to predict as accurately as possible what will happen under given circumstances. The scientific method is a way of recognizing and finding errors, even in long-held ideas. Cousins says:

> Therefore, it is unreasonable to expect physicians and other therapists to depart from this method, no matter how great the compulsion or the persuasion.

The holistic health movement can discover its greatest effectiveness by seeking balance. It would not be in the interest of the movement to regard the medical profession as the enemy. Talk of enemies does not sit well in a movement in which spiritual factors are no less vital than practical ones. Holism means healing - not just of bodies, but of relationships. One of the most useful things (any health) movement can do is to bring itself and the physician together in mutual respect for the ability of the human body to be fully potentiated in maintaining health and in overcoming disease.

I believe it is reasonable to expect a physician to respect the power of the mind in overcoming disease, especially in light of the new evidence of how our body chemistry is affected by our will or our emotional state. However, Cousins goes on to caution:

It is unreasonable to expect a physician to give those approaches a monopoly status in the care of patients and to abandon other medical methods that have already proven to be efficacious in varying degrees.

Two Important Movements

In the last half-century, two distinct yet parallel events have occurred to offer effective help to those dealing with chemical dependency and co-dependency.

1. The founding of Alcoholics Anonymous (AA) in 1935.

2. The beginning of the study of group process as described by Carl Rogers, who began working with groups in 1950 and writing about them in 1970.

> **Both movements grew up outside the establishment.**

In 1970 universities and the medical profession looked upon both movements with scorn. There were no research funds available to study these techniques, either to validate or challenge the theories behind them. Clinical psychology and psychiatry stayed aloof, as did the mainstream of medicine.

GROUP PROCESS

The John Birch Society considered encounter groups a Communist plot and only for "bohemians." Carl Rogers stated at the time that he knew of few other trends that so clearly expressed the needs and desires of the "people," rather than institutions. At the time, the popularity of therapeutically directed groups and self-help groups blossomed. The group therapy he speaks of was unstructured and undirected and was not used to treat any specific disorder or illness. Rather, in the '40s, Rogers used groups to tie together experiential and cognitive learning in a process that seemed to have therapeutic value for his patients. He learned this while training Veterans Administration counselors.

Then, in 1947, Curt Lewis, a psychologist at the Massachusetts Institute of Technology, developed the idea that training in human relations was an important and overlooked type of education, and he formed the Bethel Groups, which were the predecessors of encounter groups. The groups would choose their own goals and direction. Perhaps there would be some cognitive input; a professional facilitated the expression of thoughts and feelings of each of the members. The focus, however, was on the process and the dynamics of interpersonal interaction.

The groups provided intensity, safety, emotional freedom and immediate feelings toward each other. Many times feelings were expressed for the first time by group members. Mutual trust, open communication and feedback were encouraged. New ideas, concepts, directions and a carryover of the benefits to life outside the group were being realized.

12-Step Groups

During these critical years self-help groups (primarily Alcoholics Anonymous and Alanon) began to flourish; these have been one of the major social movements of our century. The key to the success of 12-step groups is a mutual sharing of beliefs and vulnerability and understanding of one another's thinking and feeling.

It's an extremely supportive fellowship. The fellowship is based on a series of steps designed to help people live and relate to others in a respectful way. There is a shared belief in a power greater than oneself—even if that is nothing more than the group itself, or a God as each member understands God.

Cognitive To Experiential

Heather Ashton, in her book on brain systems, says that psychotropic medications simply relieve symptoms long enough for a natural remission or a change to occur. They actually add an additional disorder to an already disordered brain.

Each of the therapeutic disciplines that this manual borrows from has a partial use in some system of the brain. Psychotropic drugs, cognitive and "talk-only" therapy have not had the power to imprint or reinforce change in the same way experiential, emotional and behavioral therapy do. Just as our predecessors had to learn many of their health-producing behaviors from their own diseases and then hand that new knowledge down to us, so might we through our own emotional infirmities be able to pass our new knowledge down to future generations.

SUMMARY

AA, Alanon and group process have survived due to public demand and have developed their own lives. The twenty-first century holds great hope for all of us in the helping professions.

The history of brain research has revealed a gradual transition from conjecture to the emergence of an anatomical and physiological approach in understanding the nervous system. Increasing specificity and specialization will bring the fields of behavioral psychology, psychology, psychiatry, social work, and medicine much closer together.

Understanding Co-Dependency

The following is a simplified description of co-dependency. For a more complete work, see: *Understanding Co-Dependency*, by Sharon Wegscheider Cruse and Joseph R. Cruse, published 1990 by Health Communications.

Dimensions of the Disease

The disease of co-dependency itself is a *current brain process*, regardless of

- gender
- past history of the individual
- the environment the individual grew up in or currently lives in.

The brain process is basically one of denial, repression and compulsion. The three dimensions of the illness are:

1. The process dimension

    The brain system disorder that can lead to a disabled spiritual life (low self-worth), a disabled social life (intimacy problems) and a disabled body (medical complications).

2. The person dimension

    There will be various treatment approaches depending on whether the patient has had previous treatment or is young or

old. It matters whether the person is skilled at self-care or not.
It's important to know if the person has a past history of
repeated treatments for other psychiatric problems. Will this
patient allow us to use diagnostic or therapeutic strategies or
will this patient resist our attempts to help?

3. The environment dimension

There will be different treatment approaches and different
follow-up, aftercare and relapse prevention strategies needed.

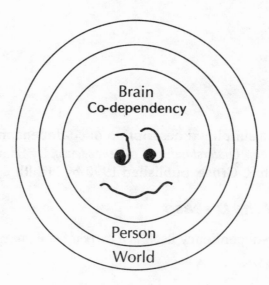

What we have here is a susceptible person living dependently in an
addictive society. A susceptible person is constantly looking for relief
and reward. He tries different substances such as alcohol, drugs, caffeine,
nicotine or sugar. He might also experiment with different behaviors
that are rewarding or relieving, such as excess work, sex, gambling,
control of others, exercise, caretaking, overeating or undereating. Society
condones and even encourages some of his dependencies.

The disease of co-dependency:

1. can be described;
2. progresses if left untreated;
3. is treatable in most cases.

Its symptoms fall into three categories:

1. delusion (denial);
2. emotional repression;
3. compulsive behaviors.

Complications also fall into three categories:

1. chronic low self-worth (damaged spirituality)
2. relationship problems (damaged socially)
3. medical problems (damaged physically)

The next chapter explores these complications.

Symptoms

Delusion

The denial/delusion that characterizes co-dependency originates in love. At some point, that love is perverted by the realization that one cannot control the feelings and responses of another (e.g., family, partner, friend). Love becomes fear, fear ultimately becomes emotional paralysis, and the paralysis soon feels like entrapment. We don't know how it happened. We started out needing to be loved, and now we are stuck.

Since recognition of our "sick relationships" would require recognition of the self as dysfunctional, the co-dependent does what he must to maintain the situation as is: he normalizes, e.g., "It' not that bad," or "It's better than it used to be."

This rationalization by the co-dependent is often deeply felt and truly believed - a "sincere delusion." Dependency is a perceived experience, one that grows out of an individual's compulsive response to something initially so effective, so self-worth-producing, and so comforting that he does not want to (can't!) be without it.

> ## *Dependence, whether on alcohol, drugs, money, food, or another person, is dependence all the same.*

Confusion about making decisions and rigid, judgmental attitudes (when everything is black or white, with no shades of gray) are expressions of the denial/delusion aspect of co-dependency.

Repression

Deep inside the individual are potentially immobilizing emotions: fear, guilt, anger, loneliness. People can work through these feelings and eventually get past them as they recover health and hope, or they can repress these feelings. Life becomes a social theater, and people wear masks. What are these individuals hiding?

- Anger
- Loneliness
- Fear
- Hurt

Anger. Often, the co-dependent's attempts to control backfire. Attempting to control someone else, a substance, or a behavior is a self-defeating project. This results in frustration, which turns to anger as things fall apart. The anger turns to rage, which is often swallowed or stuffed.

Store enough feelings, and the symptom that appears is depression. As time goes on, the mind becomes a storehouse for pent-up memories and hidden resentments. One may think these hurts have disappeared, but they have not - not after weeks, months, or even years. The chronic stress created by unresolved emotional hurts can lead to serious health problems (as we shall see later), career and marriage problems and reduced vitality.

Symptoms of repressed rage are:

- losing your temper over a small matter;
- frequently feeling disappointed and let down by others;
- not wanting to call or visit friends or relatives;
- weight problems (gaining or losing);
- chronic backaches, headaches, stomach aches, etc.

Even more regrettable is the fact that hidden anger and resentment lead to a diminished experience of love and joy throughout one's life. When one is fighting back painful feelings, current relationships are affected in a variety of ways.

> ## It is difficult to show affection for loved ones if it also feels necessary to maintain control by keeping people at arm's length.

The sad result of avoiding anger is just the opposite of what people expect. The individual is capable only of inauthentic forms of human interaction. Eventually, relationships become difficult to handle, reach an impasse, and fall apart. Hidden aggression is often unconscious and automatic; it would be denied if confronted. Often, it looks like love and care.

In addition to anger, other repressed feelings are:

Loneliness. The co-dependent feels as though nobody really understands. Feelings of differentness are nurtured by growing isolation. This fosters further loneliness and isolation.

Fear. Co-dependents live with feelings of low self-worth, believing themselves to be totally powerless.

> ## Yet efforts to get a handle on as many situations as possible result in the co-dependent becoming a controller.

The pathological need to control so much naturally results in a great deal of fear. There is fear of being found out, of not being good enough, of relaxing and letting one's guard down because things might fall apart. There is the all-consuming fear of abandonment, loneliness and rejection.

Hurt. After the individual has trapped himself in the caretaker role, it becomes expected. Family and other friends take that responsibility for granted, and this can be painful for a person who has expected at least the reward of abject gratitude for his super-responsibility. Existing to take care of others is a joyless existence, and acknowledging the trap can hurt so much that the co-dependent will resist information and feedback in order to maintain the illusion that he is needed as much as he wishes he was. Beneath the surface of many a super-responsible person is a sad, lonely, hurting one.

There are many more feelings (loneliness, shame, jealousy, inadequacy, etc.) that need to be recalled, refelt and discharged. Without expression, these feelings lead to a reservoir of painful feelings that trigger a craving for relief that leads to compulsion.

COMPULSIVE BEHAVIOR

Compulsive behavior can be expressed in the seeking of relief from emotional pain by using outside substances; e.g., alcohol, drugs, nicotine, sugar, and caffeine.

A rush of internal chemicals can also offer some relief. The following behaviors release chemicals that give us temporary, short-term rushes of relief/reward from emotional pain:

> controlling/caretaking
> sexual acting out
> relationship dependency
> gambling
> workaholism
> eating disorders
> excessive exercise

> # Among the forms of compulsion, we encounter people who live their lives in response to others' expectations.

As children, spouses, lovers and parents, such people's *raison d'etre* is to figure out others' wants and deliver them. This is a trap of paradox. It requires the most sophisticated skills in manipulation and control; yet the person ends up quite controlled and manipulated himself.

Additional examples of compulsive behavior are: people who need to control themselves and others; people who lie and exaggerate when it would be just as easy to tell the truth, and approval-seeking in its many forms. This kind of people-pleasing is clearly self-destructive.

> ## Delusion, repression and compulsion are major co-dependency symptoms that must be addressed in experiential treatment.

If these symptoms are not addressed, complications of co-dependency can develop, as happens with many diseases.

Complications

Three major groupings of complications occur in co-dependency.

> ## Complications are a result of the disease, and should not be confused with its causes.

LOW SELF-WORTH

All family systems can be measured on a continuum between painful and healthy. The healthier the family system, the higher the self-worth of the individuals in that system. The more painful a family is, the more low self-worth the family members suffer. Painful family systems that lower self-worth are characterized by:

- Implied "no-talk" rules;
- Internalization of feelings;
- Unspoken expectations;
- Entangled relationships;
- Control of each other;
- Ambiguous values;
- Rigid attitudes;

- Submission to the rigors of traditions, regardless of individual members' attitudes toward those traditions;
- Grim atmosphere;
- Chronic illness;
- Dependent relationships;
- Jealousy

Healthy family systems that raise self-worth are characterized by:

- Open communication;
- Open expression of feelings;
- Explicit rules;
- Respect for individuality;
- Feeling of family freedom;
- Sense of spirituality;
- Flexible, changing attitudes;
- Tradition;
- Joyful atmosphere;
- Support for change and growth;
- Trust

A major goal of recovery is to return a person to a strong sense of self-worth.

RELATIONSHIP DIFFICULTIES

> # Until we have a relationship with ourselves and heal our wounded parts, it's very difficult to have a meaningful relationship with someone else.

We develop unhealthy dependencies on other people to validate ourselves, or we shy away from commitments to others. Our relationship to others is a reflection of our relationship with ourselves. We either form dependent relationships with others or we isolate ourselves and avoid others.

Relationships to family members, friends and even people at our workplace are affected by our ability to know and understand ourselves.

A meaningful mutual primary relationship with a partner is extremely difficult. We cannot have a close relationship with someone else when we don't even know ourselves.

Experiential therapy can help us to leave our rage and regrets in the therapy room and begin to heal. Our own healing then allows us to see the past in perspective. Some people have been wounded so deeply that reconciliation and forgiveness are not possible. Others, however, can see a big family picture that prevented people from being available to each other for decades, and thus forgiveness and reconciliation become much more possible.

Experiential therapy can also help us (through role play) to explore current relationships and get feedback from others.

An important part of pain and possibility in co-dependency is our sexual relationships.

In a healthy sexual relationship we have two emotionally available people who are able to connect emotionally (emotional intercourse or intimacy). When each is able to be emotionally available, each is also able to access his or her own feelings, allowing each of them to be responsible for their own sexual arousal. Therefore it's easy for each of them to reach orgasm. Orgasm is then followed by a nourishing emotional sharing (emotional afterplay). It's a meaningful experience, with the individuals eager to repeat it. We might diagram a healthy sexual relationship this way:

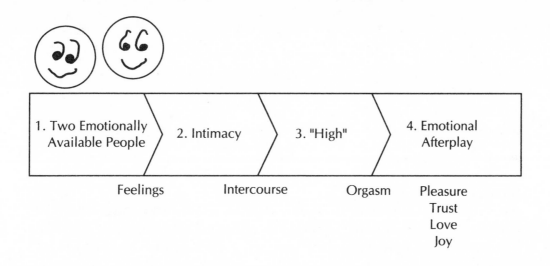

The positive feelings generated by this kind of physical sharing increase affirmation, self-worth and a general sense of well-being.

On the other hand, when one or both of the partners is co-dependent, they simply are not available emotionally to the other partner and they must depend on outside stimulation for sexual arousal. The most common stimulants are:

- masturbation
- pornography
- affairs
- seduction
- violence
- control

Needless to say, sex in this setting is not a very rich experience, and one or both partners is left very unsatisfied. It looks more like this:

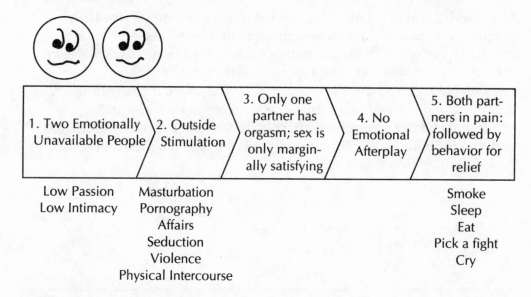

1. Two Emotionally Unavailable People	2. Outside Stimulation	3. Only one partner has orgasm; sex is only margin- ally satisfying	4. No Emotional Afterplay	5. Both part- ners in pain: followed by behavior for relief
Low Passion Low Intimacy	Masturbation Pornography Affairs Seduction Violence Physical Intercourse			Smoke Sleep Eat Pick a fight Cry

There are many sexuality issues to be explored in co-dependency treatment. They include compulsive sexual acting out and sexual abuse.

MEDICAL COMPLICATIONS

Stress-related illnesses are those whose origins can be traced to a time of particularly high or acute emotional pain. The following medical complications, though not the exclusive domain of co-dependency, do indicate that co-dependency may somehow be at work: hypochondria, anxiety, depression, insomnia, hypertension, anorexia nervosa, bulimia, colitis, bowel problems, respiratory diseases such as bronchial asthma and cardiac irregularities on a psychosomatic basis. Since sexual performance is directly related to hormonal activity, stressors can induce hormonal changes that, in turn, alter or blunt sexual performance.

SUMMARY

Treatment: See the big picture (gain perspective)
Stop the "medicators" (abstain/moderate)
Heal the feelings (re-experience)
Reduce shame (create worthiness)
Appreciate self (increase self-worth)
Draw boundaries
Invite relationships
Stay healthy

Those who understand co-dependency know:

- Recovery is a series of small changes.
- Recovery is making order out of chaos and then making changes.
- Recovery is possible.

Those in denial say:

- "Co-dependency is a fad."
- "There will never be competition in the phone system."
- "The Berlin Wall will stand forever."
- "Adult children of alcoholics won't make a difference to the addiction field."
- "Tax laws will always be the same."
- "Experiential treatment methods are a tool of a few, but not part of the mainstream."
- "No one will really fly to the moon."

As Eric Hoffer says, "In times of change, learners inherit the earth while the learned find themselves beautifully equipped to deal with the world that no longer exists."

There are many treatment models for co-dependency. We'll now describe the model that we have found very effective at our center in Rapid City.

Assessing Co-dependency

Profile Of Our Patients

In the past few years we have treated more than 2,000 patients whose primary diagnosis was co-dependency. They have come from every state in the United States and from Europe, Canada, Australia and New Zealand. Our youngest patient was 18; our oldest, 74. Both men and women have sought our help, with women slightly outnumbering men.

The program is an 8-day live-together outpatient program. Because we believe co-dependency to be a powerful disease, the program is highly structured in order to *confront* the disease and *heal* the person. The days are 14 hours long and include several hours of intensive group therapy each day.

A large majority of the patients we have treated have tested out on the Millon-MCMI-II Personality Inventory as avoidant, dependent and self-defeating personality types. Many of them also test out as histrionic and passive-aggressive and show an accompanying depression and generalized anxiety. Many of them (over 35 percent) are recovering chemically dependent individuals who also test out, well into their sobriety, as borderline sadistic-aggressive and obsessive-compulsive personality disorders. (We will explore this further in later chapters.)

Co-dependents have ingrained patterns of behaving, feeling and thinking that get reordered during experiential therapy. We are all familiar with the ego defense mechanisms we encounter in therapy. In the co-dependent population, those mechanisms differ only in degree and not in kind from those seen with other mental disorders or in the general public. They are repression, projection, displacement, denial, sublimation, regression, rationalization and reaction formation. They can all be directly addressed and treated by many of the experiential therapy exercises described in this manual.

Confrontation of the ego defense mechanisms in sculpture lends a bit of relief (frequently comic relief) to the process of confrontation that should be more enlightening than painful.

Pre-Admission Screening

Before any of our patients arrive at our center, we have gathered a great deal of information to prepare ourselves to best meet their needs. Through our extensive prescreening, using a specifically designed (for co-dependency) psycho-social questionnaire and the Millon Test (see Bibliography), we are able to determine if the patient is appropriate for our intensive 8-day treatment program. Out of the 500 patients we assess each year, 35 to 40 are referred elsewhere. Examples of patients we refer elsewhere are those with:

1. Active alcoholism or drug addiction
2. Major eating disorders
3. Accompanying psychiatric disorders, delusional, paranoid and thought disorders
4. Severe physical disabilities

Personality Traits

As we look at both the disease process and the individual, we can:

1. Study his family map to see what genetic traits he may have inherited. (Co-dependents seem to have mostly traits of novelty-seeking, harm avoidance and reward dependence.)

2. Look to see what developmental arrests may have occurred in the person's maturing years.

If a distinct disorder is present we can see where it stands in the continuum of other clinical disorders. We do not consider any personality trait a disease. We consider personality traits, however, quite ingrained and pervasive, affecting almost all the behavior, feeling and thinking that go on daily. In co-dependency we see these traits, behaviors, thoughts and emotions exaggerated so that the person becomes disordered. This can have an impact on the patient's life to the degree that he becomes disabled. Co-dependency should be regarded as a disability.

We all have co-dependent tendencies and we all have certain personality traits that we exaggerate from time to time, but when exaggerations affect a person's life on a recurring basis, the person becomes crippled mentally, physically, spiritually, emotionally and interpersonally. To effectively treat this complicated illness, we need to know exactly in what area we are working.

Co-Existing Dependencies

Different people try different substances or behavior depending on what's available to them, what is acceptable to them and what's worth the risk to them. It's probable that no one tries all the available substances and/or behaviors, but most co-dependents develop dependencies on more than one substance or behavior. We call this "co-existing dependencies." We use this and the term "co-dependency" interchangeably. We do this to keep in mind that co-dependency is more than simply a relationship issue.

Tolerance

Whenever a selection of substances and/or behaviors has been made and is working, it does not take long before our bodies (and especially our brains) play a terrible prank on us, almost guaranteeing us a disease. In this disease our behavior, our thoughts and our emotions will become extremely exaggerated to the point of actually interfering in our lives.

The prank that the brain plays on us at this time is that of "tolerance." Tolerance to exciting, anxiety-producing or even life-threatening events develops with repetition. Perhaps that is why the first promotion, the first high dive or the first time down the mountain on skis is the most exhilarating. As we proceed, the promotions must become greater, and the dives must be higher and fancier for us to get that same reward from the behavior.

This holds true in sexual acting out, gambling, caretaking, spending and eating. Tolerance is familiar to those who are addicted to alcohol, drugs, caffeine, nicotine or sugar. When tolerance builds, we have to do *more* for the same effect. More often, greater amounts, more intensity and more variety result in co-existing dependencies (co-dependency).

Reinforcement

Reinforcement is the core of operant conditioning. Based on the outcome of one's behavior (reward or relief from punishment), reinforcement more or less predicts the probability that the behavior will be repeated in the future. Certain compulsive behaviors and the use of drugs (including nicotine and alcohol) can be highly reinforcing and therefore have a high probability of being repeated.

Individuals who cope through the use of compulsive repetitive behaviors or the use of mood-/mind-altering substances, or more commonly, a combination of both, exclaim, "I found it!" The major, but not only, neurotransmitter involved in this "Eureka!" experience is dopamine, one of the brain's natural chemicals. Dopamine is a stimulant much like adrenaline. Once the "I found it!" experience hits an individual's brain, that brain is imprinted, which means the individual will not forget the result. He will repeat the process again and again, even after the process fails him. When an individual is not reinforced by a selection of substances or behaviors, he turns to other substances and behaviors until he receives relief or reward. Some substances can reinforce below the level of actual conscious mind- or mood-altering effect. Some behaviors can do likewise.

There does not seem to be a relationship between the power of reinforcement and the amount of actual mind- and mood-altering effect from any chemical or behavior. Nicotine and cocaine are equally reinforcing, although cocaine has a much greater immediate effect on the body and the emotions than does nicotine. However, both addictions are extremely difficult to break because they are so reinforcing. Reinforcement, then, is the driving force behind so many of our compulsive behaviors and substance use.

Diagnosis

The power of reinforcement and the rewards remembered are so great that it takes not only cognitive (thinking) therapy to provide information and understanding, but also experiential (emotional) therapy so that individuals can re-experience their distorted thinking and suppressed emotions, and better recognize their compulsive behaviors.

Both approaches to therapy are crucial. Cognitive therapy, which teaches the patient about the disease, is what finally breaks the denial and delusion of the patient, allowing him to surrender to the disease process. Experiential therapy is directed at the emotional pain of the patient, utilizing current and past history, his genetic makeup and personality to gain access to the actual process going on within the brain.

We diagnose patients - we give them a "label." Labeling patients is frowned upon in many quarters. However, there are many advantages to the patients if a diagnosis is handled well.

Using a diagnosis that fits the patient helps the therapists and the treatment programs to individualize specific therapy modalities and aftercare plans. Not all co-dependents have similar treatment or aftercare plans; in fact, they vary quite greatly, as will be explained later. An accurate diagnosis simplifies a complex problem.

In diagnosing patients and describing their personality traits, it is assumed that clinical behaviors will be similar if they share the same personality traits. It's also assumed that, if we have been successful with certain therapeutic techniques for a personality trait in the past, that these techniques will work in the present and for future patients. The aim of a prototypal diagnosis is to give us a clue as to what the patient has been through and what behavior we can expect. We also hope to be able to develop not only the treatment plan modeled on what has succeeded previously, but an effective aftercare plan.

There is a question as to whether categorizing patients doesn't actually impede therapy. We have found quite the opposite. (For an extensive description of the diagnosis we use with our patients at Onsite, we refer you to *Understanding Co-dependency,* Health Communications, 1990.)

Our diagnostic label and our identification of personality traits and characteristics based on observation and testing can be thought of as symbols that we use. They give order to what we are observing in a patient and sometimes lead us to information that we cannot readily see. These symbols become tools that can improve understanding between therapists and patients as well as between clinicians.

Our work in diagnosing and treating co-dependents supports our belief that co-dependency is a disease of exaggerated behaviors, emotions and thoughts, and that it may well represent a reversible stage in the development of what are now clinically recognized as Axis II personality disorders in the *Diagnostic and Statistical Manual* of the American Psychiatric Association. Co-dependency might usefully be classified as a pre-personality disorder syndrome as long as personality disorders are considered irreversible.

> ## We know that what we are seeing clinically and calling co-dependency is highly treatable and reversible.

So despite potential problems with classifications and diagnostic labels, we are increasingly supporting their use. We believe that a classification system for co-dependency simplifies the search for its relevant characteristics.

Categorization and labeling can serve as a valuable starting point for the clinician. But diagnostic categories should be used and treated as tools for further discoveries, not as a basis for academic argument. Diagnostic placement helps simplify our clinical tasks by:

- alerting us to features of the patient's history
- clarifying patient's present functioning
- enabling us to communicate more effectively with the patient

Such diagnosis also helps the patient to better understand his own illness and to use the diagnosis to better understand the treatment process and the plan for aftercare. If a diagnosis guides us to certain beneficial therapeutic techniques and puts baselines on our research design, it is certainly beneficial. Of course, any system that attempts to classify should be open and able to handle the dynamics of change and variability.

We can be most effective in treating co-dependency if we know about the severity of the presenting symptoms and complications. When we assess the patient, we are able to assess the severity of the disease and offer the most appropriate therapy.

Stages of Co-Dependency

Stages

Another advantage of accurate diagnosis is that it helps us classify a patient's co-dependency as to severity or degree of impairment. We classify the "disease process" as early, middle or late, based upon what we see in terms of denial, repression and compulsion. We classify the impairment based on the severity of the complications and how seriously disabled the individual is in his social, spiritual and physical life.

Only with a framework such as we have been describing, and by the use of diagnoses, can a classification of severity be accomplished and be consistent.

Questionnaire

In addition to the difficulty in understanding what co-dependency is all about, counselors have struggled to assess the stages of co-dependency. This has made it difficult to recommend the appropriate level of care for each person. This checklist has been helpful in that regard.

1. EARLY STAGE (WARNING SIGNS)   Check Here

    Situational loss of daily structure...................... ☐
    Lack of personal care................................ ☐
    Inability to set and stick to limits
        with children and others........................ ☐
    Loss of constructive planning...................... ☐
    Indecision .... ☐
    Compulsive behaviors............................... ☐
    Fatigue or lack of rest............................. ☐
    Return of unreasonable resentments................. ☐
    Return of tendency to control
        people, situations, things...................... ☐
    Defensiveness...................................... ☐
    Self-pity.. ☐
    Overspending...................................... ☐
    Eating disorders (over- or under-)................. ☐
    Scapegoating...................................... ☐
    Intermittent depression............................ ☐

    TREATMENTS: COUNSELING, OUT-PATIENT AND
    SELF-HELP GROUPS

2. MIDDLE STAGE (CLINICAL CO-DEPENDENCY)   Check Here

    Relapse - Return of fear and general anxiety........... ☐
    Loss of belief in a Higher Power .... ☐
    Relapse - Attendance at formal support meetings becomes
        sporadic or nonexistent........................ ☐
    Mind racing.. ☐
    Inability to construct a logical chain of thought......... ☐
    Confusion .... ☐
    Sleep disturbances .... ☐
    Uncontrollable mood swings .... ☐
    Failure to maintain interpersonal (informal) support
        systems.. ☐
    Feelings of loneliness, isolation .... ☐
    Rigidity... ☐
    Relapse - Return of periods of free-floating anxiety and/or
        panic attacks .... ☐
    Health problems.................................... ☐

Use of medication or alcohol as a way to cope . . . . ☐
Relapse - Total abandonment of support meetings, therapy
    sessions . . . . ☐
Complaints from others. . . . . ☐
Need for intervention (serious denial) . . . . ☐
Suicidal thoughts or plans. . . . . ☐

TREATMENT: 8–10-DAY RESIDENTIAL PROGRAM WITH
STRUCTURED ONE-YEAR AFTERCARE

3. LATE STAGE (DISABLING CO-DEPENDENCY)   Check Here

Inability to change behavior in spite of conscious
    awareness that it is self-defeating. . . . . ☐
Complete loss of daily structure. ☐
Despair and suicidal thoughts, plans, attempts, etc. . . . . . ☐
Major physical collapse . . . . ☐
Major emotional collapse . . . . ☐
Major social collapse . . . . ☐

TREATMENT: RESIDENTIAL 30-DAY PROGRAM WITH
STRUCTURED AFTERCARE

Treating Co-dependency

Our goals will be to:

1. Confront denial and help the patient understand, identify with and accept his co-dependency. This will be done through lectures, films, discussion and study.

2. Take the person into his emotional pain in order to lance and drain his emotional abscess. In fact, we tell patients that we need to cut and drain the toxins from their internal emotional abscess. This analogy seems readily understood by patients and helps motivate them to proceed through some painful work.

As was stated earlier, feelings are our reality. We believe that our feelings were given to us just as our other five senses were—to be used in a proper way.

But we don't always do that with our other five senses; we frequently don't do that with our feelings. We may consider feelings the sixth sense; they are the closest to reality when we say, "I have a gut feeling about that." Our emotions are chemically based in the brain and are stimulated by thoughts and especially memories. Experiential therapy can stir long-suppressed thoughts and memories. Experiential therapy allows a "refeeling" of old feelings that have remained buried and thus have had a negative effect on us—sometimes even making us physically ill.

Having all of our patients chemically free (including freedom from nicotine and caffeine) makes their feelings potentially more available to them. Skilled therapists are then able to set up and direct sculptures and psychodramas that assist the patient in accessing buried and repressed emotions. The "freeing up" and resolving of these emotions bring a dramatic emotional improvement and increase in self-worth. The return of a zest for life accompanies the resolution of buried, painful emotions.

Though this might sound like some sort of faith healing or miracle claim, it is not, for the human body is capable of healing itself, and the brain is extremely adept at handling the pain of resolution. Once the brain has done so, the momentum is difficult to stop.

We have occasionally been concerned about some of the sudden changes we have seen through the use of experiential therapy, but we have been reassured by our follow-up studies of two and four years, which indicate that most of the changes are permanent, are maintained on a mature level and therefore are productive for the individual.

Our treatment focus, as described above, is to address the disease process of *delusion, repression* and *compulsion*. Our treatment goals will address these three symptoms.

As the patient prepares to leave our center, we will address the complications of his disease (low self-worth, relationship issues and medical complications) and develop a structured aftercare plan to work through these problems.

Treatment and Aftercare Planning

The medical model allows for concise discourse between staff members and between staff members and patients. They all talk knowingly about suppression (of feelings), of their "spiritual complication," etc. Staff members frequently remind each other, especially with difficult cases: "Are we talking about the person or the disease?" Staff at Onsite present patient cases to one another at every staff meeting. They categorize these presentations by purpose:

- teaching
- consultation
- routine
- follow-up
- combination of more than one of above

Sculptures that have been used and have been particularly helpful, ineffective, modified or newly invented are also presented.

Treatment plans evolve out of these sessions, the results of the Millon Test and, of course, the patient's history. Discharge summaries include the patient's identified problems, strengths and areas on which the patient was able to work.

The aftercare plan is then developed to cover the following categories:

- continuing or initiating professional care
- continuing or initiating involvement in a 12-step self-help group
- family negotiations
- family fun
- personal care and fun
- further testing/assessment as needed
- referral to inpatient care as needed

A Note on Humor

Any treatment program that ignores the power of humor and laughter in healing and in building self-worth is incomplete. The ability to use our emotional senses includes using the sense of humor. The child within us (who is buried in the emotional abscess) deserves to be released and to be able to celebrate with laughter in play. So often the child within each of us is filled with the shame that destroys self-worth.

We have found that humor is the best antidote to shame, given its ability to return a person to a sense of self-worth. Self-worth is a spiritual quality in us. It is a requirement for possessing a zest for life. Our programs and many of the exercises in this manual lead to and can direct such therapeutic play. As Norman Cousins states, "Medicine is becoming spiritual and spirituality is becoming more important and more pervasive and is free. It costs nothing, and its rewards are so great."

> **As Jon Franklin so aptly states, "Human behavior, human emotions and human thinking are now measurably chemical, while at the same time recovery from disease is probably spiritual."**

Summary

We present a disease model based upon biopsychology as the basis for the disease itself; upon genetic and developmental theory as describing the important aspects of the person who has the disease; and upon family systems, theory and sociology as the basis for studying the environment in which the disease flourishes.

Co-dependency has been an elusive concept, but need not be. Based on the medical concept of *co-dependency as a reversible brain disorder with discrete signs and symptoms and occurring in an individual who has a unique genetic and developmental makeup,* we are able now to communicate more clearly with one another and with our patients.

The medical model and the use of experiential therapy have provided us clarity of thought regarding cause and effect and are providing specificity in our treatment strategies.

2
Experiential Therapy

Why Experiential Therapy?

Don't worry whether the sun will rise or set or whether it will rain. Just get prepared to enjoy it.

Experiential therapy blends therapies like Gestalt and family therapy with models like sculpture and role plays. The purpose is to enact or reenact the emotional climate of the family of origin and/or other past and present significant relationships in a person's life. In re-experiencing these events and relationships, one is able to release the emotions that may have been blocked and repressed.

> ## The goal is to free a person from the unresolved emotions around relationships so that he is more free to live in the present.

This is a particularly useful therapy in treating co-dependency. Two of the main symptoms of co-dependency are:

1. Blocked cognitive memory
2. Blocked, or repressed, feelings

The inability to connect with and express one's inner reality also helps create the pathology of co-dependency. By reexperiencing the emotional climate of the family, anger, shame, hurt, rage, guilt, fear, etc., can finally be expressed, released and healed, making room for feelings of love, hope, inner peace and forgiveness.

Since denial plays a big part in co-dependency, the dynamic of group experiential therapy helps to get beneath the denial as a person responds emotionally to the work of another group member. It is hard for cognitive blocking to persist in one person when emotional healing is taking place in other group members.

> ## This is one of the reasons why group work helps confront denial so much better than one-to-one sessions.

Emotions are the barometer of credibility and authenticity. They provide richness and color to life. In looking at the vast array of emotions intellectually, one knows that they are good and that all deserve to exist. Yet it is clear that some are more desirable, more pleasant, than others.

Some people have locked a whole set of emotions into a closet, to be hidden from all, to be forgotten by themselves. Frequent occupants of these locked closets are anger, loneliness, inadequacy, hurt, guilt, fear or sadness. They form almost a mob of feelings demanding attention.

Feelings are facts.

> ## Feelings, like all of reality, have a right to exist.

Reality is intolerant of denial. When feelings are repressed, they demand attention in devious ways. The emotional connection between stress and stomach problems is common knowledge. Research is showing more and more that the whole person becomes ill, not just part of the person. Consequently, emotions are similar to muscles—if you don't use them, you lose them.

> ## *In our opinion, experiential therapy is the most effective and useful tool in the healing of old pain and the developing of new possibilities.*

Experiential therapy is a treatment approach that combines theory with action. It is a technique that therapists can use to touch people's lives deeply and intimately. Its effect can be profoundly healing.

Treatment is a combination of knowledge and experience. To utilize one without the other is incomplete therapy. Many treatment centers and therapists do an excellent job of imparting the knowledge available regarding addictive diseases and co-dependency. Films, lectures and readings provide enough information so that people can go home "knowing" the dynamics of addiction and co-dependency. But it is not enough to hand a patient or client a book or handout, and say, "Read this, and be better!" It doesn't work because it's all information and little emotional healing.

People often come to therapy overloaded with knowledge, self-educated with tremendous amounts of information about addictions, compulsions and feelings. They can quote theories, cite experts, use all the right words. But it doesn't help them improve their own conditions or learn new choices.

The patient reports, "I know about denial; I know about compulsion; I know about feelings. But I still do the same kinds of things that get me in trouble." That's where actual experience - personally encountering or undergoing specific emotions and behaviors - can be helpful in breaking out of compulsion and denial. Experiential therapy offers emotional alternatives and clarity about new behaviors.

One important goal of therapy is to reexperience an old event in which the accompanying emotions were not expressed at the time. The reexperience can be an opportunity to feel those feelings now, work through them now and defuse them once and for all. The accompanying emotional pain is no longer repressed and allowed to fester.

Old feelings we often help clients reexperience are anger, inadequacy, jealousy, loss, grief and shame. In the reexperience, they are able to let the pain go, and relief begins. New feelings that are unfamiliar and often scary are feelings of contentment, serenity, hope, trust, excitement, gratitude and joy. It is important to lead clients to these new feelings. Too often, therapy only deals with pain.

In therapy, we can often lead people to these healing feelings for the first time. We see self-esteem blossom. Through interaction with others and through expressing both old and new feelings, we provide a means for people to develop an ability to trust, as well as insight leading to new choices and a sense of inner comfort.

> ## We habilitate and we rehabilitate. We help equip people with social and emotional skills they have never possessed.

In a painful family system, words and messages are confused, confusing and incongruent. Words are misused and messages mistrusted. Actions do not fit. These are the double messages delivered over and over and received each time with confusion and shame. The resulting confusion is devastating and produces people of chronic low self-worth.

> ## Experiential therapy can expose double messages by leading people to discover their own emotions and to see the roles others play.

We even teach a language to help people understand what they are feeling. Usually there are few feelings that people can share. Anger is one of the few emotions that people can identify, but confusion abounds even here. For some, anger equals rage. To be angry means, to them, to be hostile, screaming, abusive or rejecting. They can't understand that sarcasm and irritation are also expressions of anger. They accept this anger as normal behavior.

Rage reduction includes encounter bat work and screaming. Anger work includes confronting and exposing sarcasm, passive/aggressive behavior (being late, imposing on others, caustic humor, forgetting, controlling). Do not be afraid to use the bats, but also do not hide behind them and forget to confront subtle and damaging "clever" anger.

So one goal of experiential therapy is to provide people with the knowledge of a "feeling language."

1. *The Compulsive Talkers:* These are the verbal, articulate, bright types who just talk too much, and in so doing, medicate their feelings. We have developed a tool called "the shoulder salute." It is a kind way of drawing attention to the compulsive talker without adding to the words. Prearrange the meaning of the shoulder salute and, when someone goes off into the "verbal maze" gently put your hand on his shoulder. It's a clue to just stop and register the feeling.

> **Experiential therapy is good with talkers because, put simply, it forces them to be quiet and pay attention to what is really going on.**

It prevents them from hiding behind their own words.

Family Heroes (the articulate leaders) benefit from experiential therapy because it forces them out into the open, unlike talk therapy, where they feel safe and can use their verbal skills to avoid taking risks.

2. *The Silent Ones:* These are the frightened people, so uncomfortable and unsophisticated with words that they have difficulty expressing themselves.

One can set up a sculpture and people can act out their roles and emotions, giving the therapist a tremendous amount of information and insight.

Experiential therapy is done in the context of a sharing session with feedback. It's less important to have lots of information *prior* to a sculpture. Often, words dilute the process. It's extremely important to gather and process feedback *after* the sculpture in order to be clear about the feelings felt and the lessons learned.

The primary aim of experiential therapy is to have the client address a particular issue, memory, compulsion, event, etc.—whatever it is that is causing conflict or struggle. Two helpful methods are frequently used: looking for the opposite and exaggerating the obvious.

1. *Look for the opposite.* Pick a defense that needs correcting, for example. Identify its opposite, its antidote, and seek it out.

   Withdrawal is a common defense among some members of painful families. In a group, ask the withdrawn person to ask three fellow group members for their help in changing a behavior pattern. This enforced interchange is a way to confront withdrawal.

   For someone who is shy, this is extremely difficult to do. It is frightening to ask for help. We are trying to move the client away from one defense by unfolding an opposite experience— asking for help. And, in asking for help, the client discovers more self-worth and some courage. Simple to describe, difficult to do.

   For a person who talks instead of feels, run a "listening exercise" with some kind of reporting back to the group. This is helpful without being "shaming." For the person who is hostile, make them the "care giver" for the group, giving neck rubs, arranging chairs, pillows, etc.

2. *Exaggerate the obvious.* This can be fun and therapeutic at the same time. This is effective with the family member who is the family organizer. This person overly commits, gives care in every situation, accepts too many demands—someone who doesn't say "no."

   Have this person identify and describe the sources of demands upon him: husband, wife, kids, job, family of origin, exercise class, church, support groups, etc. Have people role-play these, and have them make all their demands at once, in a babble of noise and confusion.

Instruct the client to confront and negotiate each demand. This experience of saying "no" and renegotiating may be totally new.

Exaggerating the obvious is also effective in working out loss and pain that may have been suppressed for years. Hurting people suffer enormous losses. They may not even be aware of their own sadness and hurt. Some losses may be the loss of people (death, divorce, moving away, major difference). Some might be loss of self (childhood, teen years, parenthood, etc.). The pain from these losses may never have been addressed.

Ask the person to act out his pain by telling the departed whatever he feels he needs to say. Have the others in the group personify that which is departed, the cause of the pain, and reply to the client. The experience is emotional, cleansing and healing.

A similar experiential technique can be applied to a client with low self-worth. Ask the group to recall thoughts or messages that were received or desired as a child. For healthy people, this is easy, but for unhealthy people, it can be difficult. This has to do with affirmations.

Experiential therapy may offer some people the opportunity to re-experience forgotten or repressed parts of their lives that may have been unavailable to them for a long period of time; for others, experiential therapy may provide the first opportunity to feel some feelings. Either way, by gaining the experience, they acquire the means to better cope with life. They are then ready to learn new experiences they can use to continue on the road to growth and recovery.

The acceptance of experiential therapy has been slow. Many therapists, especially supervisors and directors of programs, have been hesitant to look at, study and implement a new way of doing things.

> # *Dedication to the "tried and true" is always easier and safer than breaking new ground and taking risks.*

Yet, over the past few years, as more and more professionals have expanded their knowledge and experience to include new and innovative therapeutic methods, there seems to be a critical mass developing. Today experiential therapy is entering the mainstream. What was quite rare twenty years ago is beginning to get a foothold in many traditional settings.

Knowing how to evaluate our work in co-dependency has been greatly enhanced by a tool we have developed at Onsite called "the TUMSS method."

The TUMSS Method

Therapy that utilizes experiential methods has often been called magical and even mysterious. Therapists and patients both report healing that is felt deeply and followed by significant behavior change. Learning experiential skills has often required long apprenticeships or on-the-job observation.

Rather than being a technician using one clearly defined therapeutic method, experiential therapists tend to use many kinds of models, themes, or skills. Such therapists have often been trained in many modalities and are able to use whichever one fits the situation. In this sense, they can become an artist who blends trainings (Gestalt, psychodrama, group skills, TA, behavior modification). As my friend "Big Dog" says, "It's like having many colors in your paint box and being able to paint a full, rich picture, not limited to one or two roles."

In order to better understand the uses of and reasons for many of the tools used in experiential therapy, we developed an evaluation tool that has been highly useful in our co-dependency treatment program. It is known as the TUMSS method of evaluation. Each exercise is "tumss'ed" for its appropriateness and usefulness.

Using the TUMSS method of evaluating group effectiveness has been a valuable asset to our staff meetings. The therapists learn from each other and can offer helpful suggestions to each other to further enhance group work.

T = Title/Technique
U = Uses
M = Mechanics/Method
S = Simulates
S = Stimulates

So much group work has previously been hard to evaluate, quantify or teach. With the TUMSS method, communication becomes easier and more clear.

"The TUMSS Method" and our style of experiential therapy are taught each summer in our training institute.

Onsite Training Institute

This manual was developed for use in Onsite's professional training institute. The experiential group therapy taught there is one of the most effective tools available for treating co-dependency. The Onsite Institute offers training in sculpting, psychodrama and other experiential techniques. The schedule includes:

- Teaching about co-dependency and adult child issues
- Classes and discussion on intimacy, couples, sexuality, relationships, smoking, forgiveness, and sexual abuse
- Classes and workshops focusing on skill development in experiential group therapy, sculpture, communication, developing self-worth, family-of-origin work, and the use of humor and play in a therapeutic setting

The institute's experiential training track is open to counselors, physicians, and other helping professionals. Applicants must have at least a degree in an appropriate field or be certified alcoholism counselors.

The institute is a professional training workshop only. Small-group sessions involve techniques and exercises, with participants involved in demonstrations. However, no personal therapy is done. Other programs at Onsite address treatment needs.

Workshops are held in Rapid City, South Dakota. For more information, write or call Onsite Training and Consulting, Inc., 2820 West Main Street, Rapid City, South Dakota 57702, (605) 341-7432.

DISCLAIMER

This manual is intended for the use of trained professionals. The exercises contained herein are effective and powerful when used in the proper setting, with the proper indications and by experienced professionals. This manual was written for those who are trained to work in group therapy and on co-dependency issues. Gestalt and psychodrama training are helpful disciplines for using these exercises.

This manual is not a "do-it-yourself" book. The written text may be quite helpful to many educators, but the experiential exercises are inappropriate for individuals' self-use or for 12-step self-help groups or any other support groups who do not have professionally trained leaders.

Onsite disclaims any responsibility for the outcome of the use of any of these exercises.

TUMSS Exercises

Group Openers

Critic And Cheerleader

1. To gather current data
2. An "icebreaker" in the group process

Take two empty chairs and write the word "Critic" on a card and "Cheerleader" on another; tape one on each chair. Then invite group members to sit facing the two empty, labeled chairs. One at a time, have each person sit first in the critic's chair and share what he doesn't like about himself. Then have each person sit in the cheerleader's chair and share what he likes about himself.

Therapist's Note: Processing should be done after a person has sat in each chair; personalizing the sharing (e.g., "I am always apologizing for everything") makes the delivery system more powerful.

The "critic and cheerleader" can be used to help with the patient who seems stuck or resistant. Bring the critic and

81

cheerleader up after the work is stopped. Have the cheerleader encourage the patient and have the critic say things like "Don't listen to this group leader." These conflicting voices will challenge the participant in ways that will enable the work to resume.

The "critic and cheerleader" can also be used as a surprise "spot check" to see how the client evaluates the work he is doing (e.g., Cheerleader: "I believe you are courageous for the commitment to take these risks." Critic: "None of this will ever help you - you are never going to change." Which voice is the patient listening to?).

 Messages to the self.

 Awareness of the invasiveness of negative messages, self-worth and group bonding. Also awareness of how one internalizes experiences.

"Am I sitting on the fence waiting for someone to choose for me?"

The Front Page

1. To gather additional data on client
2. Useful as an "icebreaker" in group
3. To begin self-disclosure process

Hand patients newspaper-sized sheets of white paper and invite them to stand, hold the paper in front of them and share their "headlines." Variation can be used here; for example: patient can share an opinion (an editorial), perhaps a joke (comics section), or maybe something buried inside that no one ever reads or sees, e.g., what do you advertise? etc. The patients can also be paired off to share with each other, or one sheet of paper might be used and passed to others after one has shared.

Client attitudes, beliefs and priorities

Group closeness and self-awareness

"I celebrate the good news that I can share all of my self with others."

Green Paper Piece

Opens avenues of self-disclosure and explores individual's value systems

With group members in a circle, the therapist hands each person a plain green piece of construction paper and instructs the members to tear the paper into a shape that would best describe their relationship with money. (Leave the creative process open to the group members, but examples of what they may create are a very small "dollar bill," a large circle, a tiny circle, a house, a triangle, a mountain, etc.

When all the members have created shapes, invite them to share, one at a time, what they made and what it means to them. (Therapist needs to assure the group that there is no "right or wrong" with whatever value they share.) Once this part is completed, instruct each group member to pass his value to the person on his right.

With the new values that they have in their hands, invite group members to share what that symbol means to them. It may have nothing to do with what the previous owner just shared about that shape. Also have them share what it is like to have that value forced on them. (It's important for the therapist at some point to remind the group that values are not written in stone, and consequently some people may like the new shape better than the one they created, etc.)

Once this part is completed, have the group members pass the shapes back to the left so that the individuals now have their original shapes. Challenge members to answer the following question for themselves: "Does this shape represent their recovery?"

Individual values and ownership

Awareness about values in general and how they relate to one's personal recovery process.

"My values can always be reframed, altered, modified, discarded, exchanged and celebrated."

Perfect Self

Guided imagery so patient can visualize and experience his full, cohesive self and the joy of recovery

With a tape of a rainstorm playing softly in the background, have group members relax, lie on floor and visualize themselves walking through a city in the rain and pausing to take shelter in a museum. Bring the tape volume down and have the group members experience walking into the museum, taking off their raincoats, closing their umbrellas, etc. and starting to explore all the different works of art (paintings and sculptures).

At some point, have the group members focus on a particular sculpture at the end of a long room. As they get closer to the sculpture, each member realizes that this is a sculpture of his perfect self.

Ask group members to take a "mental photograph" of what it looks like, what pose it is in, what its base is like, what the sculpture is wearing, what its facial expression is, what is written on the base of the statue, etc. Then have him invite this sculpture down off the base to have a celebration dance.

As the group members each continue to experience the "perfect self," have each memorize feelings that he may have. Bring the dance slowly to a close and have the "perfect self" say good-bye, climb back up on the base and wink playfully.

Now lead group members from the room knowing that they can return to this "perfect self" anytime they wish. Continue to lead group members back out of the museum, and gather the raincoats and umbrellas. Have them go back out into the rainstorm, bring the tape volume up and bring the imagery to a close.

Therapist's Note: Sometimes it is very helpful at the close of this piece to have the individual draw his "perfect self" and share that with the group.

Recovery goals and unconditional love

Feelings of love, self-acceptance, hope and nurturance

"Do I believe there is something I can do to make me love myself more - or do I love myself just the way I am?"

T
Title/Technique

Share a Prop

 U
Uses

1. A good "icebreaker" to start group process
2. Excellent vehicle to obtain information about each person and emotional temperature

 M
Mechanics/Method

Place all props in the middle of the group circle and have each member select a prop that represents his history with co-dependency. Next have each share his selection and feelings.

Therapist's Note: A way to help the group discharge feelings here would be to have one member adorn himself with the props after all have shared and release their feelings towards "the disease."

 S
Simulates

Current relationship with the disease process

 S
Stimulates

Self-disclosure, awareness and discharge of feelings

"It is time for me to get a handle on my disease. Help me—we are in this together."

Energizers

Affirmation Chant

Promotes self-worth

Have group members sit in a circle holding hands; have them close their eyes and think a loving thought about themselves. Then, on the count of three, have them open their eyes and shout those affirmations as loud as they can. Have them continue to repeat them, each time getting a little softer, until they are just a bare whisper. Then have group members think them silently.

Therapist's Note: This exercise is a great energizer and takes only a few minutes to do. Make sure participants know to make eye contact with others as they continue to chant, bring the volume down and the message quietly home.

Self-talk

Energy, self-esteem and bonding

"It is more important for me to tell me who I am than for me to tell the world who I am."

Associations

 Group energizer

 Have each group member write a word on a card and then, one at a time, have them pass their words to the person on their left. The member receiving the word has to stand and act out the first thing that the word brings to mind. After this is done, he passes the card to the person on his left, who continues this until all have shared. Then invite another person to pass his word to the person on the left and keep the process rolling.

Therapist's Note: Sometimes interesting data and images can be obtained for use in later group process.

 Brain and life events

 Childhood playfulness and creates bonding

"One reason I am in recovery is so I can have problems and not a disease."

The Circus

Energizer for group process

Therapist announces to the group that they are now under "the big top" and invites people one at a time to become members of the circus in a role of their choice. Each patient may use movement, verbiage, etc. to act out this role. This is an additive process; once it is completed, freeze the sculpture and invite individuals one at a time to view what's been created.

The therapist should also encourage sharing as there may be some roles that are more attractive to other group members, some that are scary, and some that may remind them of their dysfunctional home lives.

Therapist's Note: Once they have shared, I have also asked the group members to switch roles and repeat the process.

Childhood playfulness and personal pathology

Feelings, identification and memories

"Learning can be fun. I have the willingness to challenge myself."

Deathstyle Dances

1. Energizer for group process
2. Understanding of co-dependency life events

With group members in a circle, invite them to show the other group members a new dance with the understanding that these new dances of choice are "co-dependency dances." It is a good idea for the therapist to begin by teaching a dance (e.g., "I'm teaching the dance of the hyperactive, noisy co-dependent"). Therapist will get in the center of the circle and proceed to teach this spontaneous dance. The other group members will duplicate this in this outside circle. When the dance is finished, the therapist then selects another person who gets in the middle and continues the process.

Therapist's Note: It may be useful to refer to one of these dances as the treatment process continues to help animate a patient's sculpture.

Brain and life events of untreated co-dependency

Fun and promotes integration of co-dependency concepts in a non-threatening way; also helps to energize and bond the group

"My deathstyle was a dress rehearsal. The curtain was lifted. Now I have a lifestyle."

Hunter and Hunted

1. Group energizer and bonding exercise
2. A method to gain additional data

Divide the group in half and instruct one half that they are "hunters" and the other half are "the hunted." Next, have one hunter circle one of the hunted (sitting in middle of room). Have this hunter share who he is, what he feels and thinks, what weapons he uses when hunting, etc.

As the hunter continues to circle "the hunted," freeze "the hunter" and have "the hunted" person share what animal he is, what he feels and thinks, where he is going to hide, etc. When this information is provided, have the two reverse their roles and repeat the process.

Upon completion, have the people share what they experienced in playing the two contrasting roles. Repeat until each group member has been hunted and been a hunter.

Therapist's Note: Sometimes anger release becomes part of this process so the encounter bat should be handy.

Passive and aggressive associations

Awareness and frozen feelings

"What am I looking for and what am I finding?"

I'm a Hundred Bees

An energizer for group process

Have group members in a circle. Therapist explains that members can select any noun they want and that they will animate this noun with their bodies and voices in an exaggerated way. Therapist then gets in the center of the circle and says for example, "I'm a hundred bees" and proceeds to make buzzing noises and move his body in hyperkinetic manner.

When this "dance" is complete, therapist points to another group member, who will then get in the circle and become 100 of something else. The process is continued until everyone has shared.

At the close of this piece, I have found it helpful for everybody to do the "dance" that they selected all at once. This adds even more to the energy flow of the group and to the sense of fun the exercise creates.

Child's safe environment

Fun, creativity and spontaneity in group process

"It is safe for me to be spontaneous and I find pleasure in playtime."

I Want to Hold Your Hand

1. To energize group process in a nurturing way
2. To enable learning more about co-dependency

With soft music playing, have group members sit in a circle and hold hands. Have each group member place his left hand on the right knee of the group member on the left. Have group members start giving love and nurturing to their partners' hands. Have the group members do this with their eyes closed so that they are all experiencing giving love.

Have them explore every aspect of the hand, the softness of the skin, the elastic nature of it, the wonder of all the bones in the wrist, the thumb, the tips of the fingers, all the different textures, etc., and then provide this "zinger." Say to them: "The untreated co-dependent's problem is not so much that he cannot give love, but that he cannot receive love. I want to ask you right now, what hand are you concentrating on?" This often evokes laughter and also imprints awareness of co-dependency.

Active co-dependency in a safe, nurturing environment

Bonding, learning trust and touching that will energize the group process

"To myself I say: how do I love thee, let me count the ways."

If Your House Could Talk

1. Energizer for group process
2. Safe vehicle for group members to begin refeeling generalized anxiety
3. Challenges the "no-talk rule"

Have group members sit in a circle and, one at a time, stand and put themselves in a still pose that would best describe the house in which they grew up. Then have them say, "If your house could talk, what would it be saying right now?" Once this has gone all the way around the room, conclude this piece by processing what has been shared.

Childhood losses and/or abuse

Expression of loss, grief, hurt and anger

"Recovery is not about fixing a hole in the roof or painting a wall. It is about tearing the house down and building a new one."

The March

 Energizer for group process

 Children love to march. Therapist selects the music, e.g., John Phillip Sousa. I like to play the first record I ever purchased, Johnny Horton's "The Battle of New Orleans", and teach the group some simple choreography to help people march along with the music.

Therapist's Note: A piece like this is very helpful as a "spacer" between chunks of heavy patient work during group process.

 Child's safe environment

 Playfulness, group bonding and energy

"I celebrate my recovery one day and one step at a time, and play is part of my recovery."

Walks

1. To energize group process
2. Introduces movement and role-playing to new group members

With soft music playing, invite the group members to stand and begin to explore the room and make friends with their "space." Do this in a series of walks that will be interpreted. Invite them to show, nonverbally, what it's like to walk in the rain. Continue this by stopping the walks and starting them again with other dance suggestions such as walking through the snow, what it's like to "walk" happy, sad, angry or busy.

Freeze the piece at this point and have group members close their eyes; ask them to be aware of anything they are feeling. Now show what it is like to walk with mother, stop that; what it's like to walk with father, stop that; finally, what it's like to walk with a higher power.

At the conclusion of these walks, turn the music off and have the group members sit down and process any new awareness that they may have received, any similarities in the walks, etc.

Childhood and contemporary emotional patterns

Body awareness, old frozen feelings and bonding in the group

"Nothing much can grow in the dark. I am walking into the light."

T

Title/Technique

War Cry

U

Uses

1. Energizer for group process
2. Identifies the "warrior" inside each group member

M

Mechanics/Method

Put on a tape of Native American war chanting. Invite the group to stand and allow the music to "enter their spinal cords." Therapists should then share his own "war cry" in the center of the group. Then invite group members, one at a time, to join him in the center of the circle to create another, tighter circle as individuals, one at a time, share their war cries.

Therapist's Note: The "war cry" can be used as a reference point if an individual finds himself "shutting down emotionally" later on in the group process.

S

Simulates

The "tribalness" of the group

S

Stimulates

Personal power and togetherness. (This builds as all group members share their war cries and join the "inner circle."

"My power dwells within. I use my power to make choices and protect myself."

Bonding

Cards

1. Bonding exercise for group
2. Introduces role-playing to group members
3. Provides learning about compulsions in a safe manner

Therapist has note cards on which are written outside chemical or behavioral medicators that activate our internal chemicals, e.g., alcohol, drugs, sugar, nicotine, work, sex, eating, caretaking. Therapist invites group members to randomly select a card and, one at a time, role-play (either verbally, nonverbally, by using movement or by putting their bodies in a still sculpture) the medicator that they have selected.

Therapist's Note: This exercise usually starts out as "fun" and eventually leads to the sharing of emotional pain as group members begin to identify with the medicators.

Brain events (distorted behaviors) of co-dependency

New understanding of medicators (chemical and behavioral) through imprinting; also provides opportunity to explore the devastating impact of distorted behaviors

"The disease is the same, the people are different."

Magic Clay

1. Provides a comfortable way to share self in group
2. A bonding exercise for the group process

Therapist has group members in a circle and reaches behind himself to pull out an imaginary ball of clay (about as big as a basketball). The therapist then explains to the group, "We are going to create some shapes and I'm going to pass the 'clay' to the group member on my left, who will create something. When he finishes, pass it on until we've completed the whole circle and the clay has come back to me.

The therapist then hands the ball to the person on his left and the process begins. Therapist should notice if the amount of clay used changes; if the volume stays the same; if shapes get added to or destroyed when it is passed along. When people receive the clay, are they getting a present or is a "bomb" being dropped on them? What type of three-dimensional shape is produced by the group members?

Therapist's Note: In my experience a well-bonded group keeps the volume of magic clay the same, and the group members create their own sculptures, as opposed to adding to what was handed to them.

Child's safe environment

Creativity and fun as well as individual and collective process awareness

"All ideas I learn are cheerful invitations to grow."

Metamorphosis

1. Promotes group bonding
2. Promotes self-disclosure
3. Identifies needs non-verbally

Line group members up and have them tell their stories non-verbally of 1) where they came from 2) where they are now and 3) where they'd like to be. This can be done all at once or one person at a time or both, back to back.

Personal history, dreams and goals

Awareness and direction for the future

"Change is life, and life and recovery happen at the same time."

Pillow Talk

1. Provides bonding with group members
2. Gives individuals an opportunity to share their medicators (good teaching sculpture to explain the disease process)

Have each group member hold a pillow, which represents his repression. At the count of three, have them all toss the pillows in the air and shout aloud that they have medicated their repressions. Then have them catch their pillows again. Repeat this several times, and then add: "This is what is so insidious about the disease of co-dependency; we can't carry it and we don't know how to get rid of it either."

Therapist's Note: Sometimes it is helpful to take two group members aside at the completion of this piece and have them continue to toss and catch their pillows, while trying to carry on a conversation with the individual facing them. This usually promotes laughter and humor. It also shows that this is what it is like to have relationships when we use compulsions to medicate our repressions. At best, we have a perforated relationship, only to be eclipsed by the compulsion itself.

Real situation with medicators and repression

Group sharing, bonding and closeness while aiding awareness of the disease process.

"I first must identify my medicators if I'm going to take the first step."

Standing on a Sheet

Can be a group theme piece or personal piece to heighten awareness and promote group bonding

Have a sheet spread out on the floor, and have group members surround the edge. Now invite a group member to stand in the middle of the sheet and share what his space represents, why he needs his space, who invades his space, who he'd invite in and why, what it feels like to claim his space, etc. Continue with each group member and process the work.

Sense of place, safety and boundaries

Insight and explores frozen and current feelings of self-worth

"This is my time and this is my space."

Stuff Your Feelings

To provide vehicle for bonding, discharge and energy awareness

Have each group member stand in a circle while holding a pillow. Invite them to share, one at a time, a feeling or an event that they have stuffed. Upon sharing, have them toss the pillows into the center of the circle.

Once the entire group has done this, explain that the stuffing of feelings and experiences creates blocks in relationships. Then have the group members lean forward and collectively push down on the pile of pillows. The therapist then becomes a "football coach" and challenges the group to "push harder and harder until the pillows are flat to the floor." Once this is done, tell the group to freeze, and then say, "This represents the amount of energy it takes to stuff your feelings."

Repression

Awareness and relief

"Rainbows are painted with all the colors in my paint box."

Touching Circles

1. Provides a comfortable way to share self
2. Good bonding exercise
3. Begins self-disclosure process

Divide the group into two circles. Have both circles touch like a figure eight; then instruct one circle to start moving clockwise and the other counterclockwise.

Therapist puts on "oldie-but-goodie" music and people begin to dance as they move in their circles. Therapist will stop music and freeze the circles.

The two group members who are now standing where the circles touch will face each other and share something about themselves. Therapist then puts music back on and circle dance continues until all group members have had a chance to share.

A child's safe environment in which group members can "check out" risk-taking

Trust, bonding, courage, self-worth, relief as well as celebration and fun for the recovery process

"When I reach out and touch someone I am touched and filled. No longer am I going to be starved for touch."

Walls and Bridges

1. Helps people share information with group
2. Helps shy individuals to begin bonding with group
3. Validates defenses and recovery risk

Divide group into halves. Have one half be Walls and the other half Bridges. Begin by having each person representing Walls stand and momentarily role-play a defense or "wall" that has kept them from feeling their pain and having relationships. Then have the Bridges stand and momentarily role-play a "bridge," i.e., an expression of ways that they have found or created to bring about healthy connections in their lives.

When this is finished, have the Walls and Bridges switch roles and continue with the process until its conclusion. At the end, invite individuals to share and process any new awareness they may have received.

Therapist's Note: Challenge group members to use their bodies in new ways. Try connecting the Walls and Bridges, etc.

Reality

Body awareness, cognitive awareness and connection through risk-taking in the group process

"Do I need excuses for not recovering or reasons for my recovery?"

The Weather Report

1. Provides a comfortable way during treatment week to share feelings and concerns about returning home
2. Good bonding exercise for the group
3. Closure piece

Hand group members a sheet of paper and have them draw a frame around the borders of the page. Tell group members that what they see in front of them is a television set and that it's time for a "weather report." Have the participants draw a picture of what they believe the emotional weather will be like for them when they return home. Patients may use whatever colors they want; at the end of their drawing invite them to share what they have drawn.

A good way to close this piece is to have group members stare one more time at their "screens," then close their eyes and visualize turning the TV off, until all they see is a blank screen.

Projection process of patient

Diffuses fear and centers patient back in the present

"When I seek to see the future, I lose my faith. When I plan for my future, it is because I have faith."

Teaching/Awareness

Advocate/Devil's Advocate

1. For patients who show signs of being stuck and confused
2. Can be used as a piece in itself or added to a sculpture already in progress

Select two members: one to play Advocate (to encourage the patient's recovery) and one to play Devil's Advocate, to reinforce the patient's indecisiveness and even to challenge the therapist, e.g., "Don't listen to that therapist, I know what is best, stay stuck and numb, listen to me."

Therpist's Note: A rope can be used with an Advocate and a Devil's Advocate on each end, with patient in middle holding on and feeling torn by the bombardment of contradictory messages.

The powerlessness of patient and his lack of choice

Awareness, choice, access to feelings and possible discharge of repressed feelings

"My confusion now means it is time for me to choose."

Anti-Social Piece

A teaching sculpture for patients who cross boundaries and project their rage

Have two group members hold piece of rope about chest-high in front of patient. On the other side of the line from the patient, have a group member role-play somebody or something the patient desires (e.g., relationship, recovery, etc.). Instruct the patient to reach out for what he desires and take a step forward.

As soon as the patient hits that line (which represents a boundary), freeze the sculpture and have another group member come from behind the patient, who is frozen with arms outstretched, stand between the patient and the sculpture, make an angry face and hold two fists up. Repeat this a few times before imparting the concept, which is that the patient crosses boundaries and projects his rage.

Therapist's Note: Patient needs to be made aware that his projection colors his perceptions; this only creates more distance in relationships.

Self-defeating style of anger, rejection and resentment

Awareness coupled with the important idea that patients must explore ways to be direct and ways to connect emotionally; they must begin to ask for what they need if their needs are going to be met

"If I don't know what my needs are, they'll never get met."

Art Gallery

1. Breaks through denial
2. Accesses repressed feelings
3. Illustrates pain (especially good for patient who seems stuck)

Give patient a large marker and have him draw on sheets of poster board. Therapist will suggest a relationship area, and patient will draw marks of choice that best represent his feelings about the relationship. (I have found it helpful to have patient make sounds as he draws to help access his feelings.)

When the drawings are completed, have group members hold them and have patient share reasons for drawing what he did with person holding the picture. When feeling needs to be released, have patient make the sounds and movements used when drawing.

Therpist's Note: This works well when done in two separate sessions - first the drawing and then the art gallery "showing."

Internal reality

Self-expression and awareness

"I refuse to be framed by my disease. I am free to exhibit my past and thus be freed of it."

Distancing

To bring awareness to group member who exhibits little or no participation, or who connects with other group members in superficial ways

Have patient stand on one side of the room. Therapist stands in the middle of the room and remaining group members line the far wall.

Therapist explains to group members that they are to mark off with their bodies how close they feel to the patient standing alone on the other side, i.e., if they feel 100 percent close to the patient they are to walk up and put a hand on the patient's shoulder. If they don't feel close at all, they are to stay right where they are, etc. (Reminder here: therapist should tell the group members that when they are marking off the distance to represent how close they feel to the patient; not how close they would like to feel to the patient. After this work is completed, some processing may be in order, or it may be time to move into a piece of work for the patient who is receiving this awareness.

Real-life situation and the patient's exaggerated style of evasiveness and avoidance

Awareness and possible motivation

"Sometimes a lightning bolt is all the light I need."

The Empty Self

Explores needs and identifies what did not happen in one's early development

With the group members scattered around the room, have each person share one thing his parents did that had a negative impact during childhood. When everyone has shared, have members now whisper the opposite of what they just shared (i.e., what they deserved) and then bring them to the center of the room one at a time. For example, if one said, "My father was never home on the weekends," he would whisper next, "I deserved to be loved and made special." Have them continue to whisper their needs (in the present tense) as they are clustered in the middle of the room. Keep tightening the group and build the whisper to a loud chant. When the chant peaks, have the group freeze and say "what you have heard from each other and felt together is an example of a full and cohesive self."

Whole person by sharing and joining parts

Awareness, self-worth and bonding

"Sometimes it's not what happened, but what didn't happen. I didn't get much when I was growing up."

The Expert Hour

To promote self-worth and fun by connecting with "inner child"

Have group members think of something they wanted to do or become as a child, e.g., cowboy, ballet dancer. Create a "Tonight Show" environment in room and have each group member come "on stage" as that person and share. Therapist acts as the talk show host. Continue this until each group member has been in the "spotlight," then process this experience.

The childlike part of self

Playfulness and validation of self

"I am an expert because I've learned from me."

Excess Baggage

1. Breaks through participant's denial
2. Provides awareness of what participant is bringing into relationships
3. For individual or couples work

Have participant gather his "excess baggage" (old fears, relationships, broken dreams, resentments) and string them all together, using yarn or rope. Use group members to role-play the baggage. Have the participant pull and drag it around the room as he tries to establish a relationship with other group members. Participant becomes exhausted as the energy of the past and unfinished business drain him. Many large pillows and props can be used.

Loss of energy and choices

Anger, frustration and powerlessness

"I am ready to do life, instead of doing time."

Fall In Love

Teaching sculpture to illustrate unhealthy choice-making in the selection of partners

Select two individuals to stand in front of group. Cover each with a sheet and put music tape on (for example, Patsy Cline's song, "I Fall to Pieces"). Let the two people try to find each other and then dance with the sheets obstructing their views. This provokes laughter, but the point is that each one is having a relationship with disease, disease to disease.

Freeze the sculpture, then have one person remove the sheet and have them dance again. Explain that this is what recovery is like in couples when one is getting healthy and the other remains the same. There are only two choices here; either the other partner will get into recovery too or the recovering person will slip back into what we call "recovery guilt" and resume his pathology.

Next, remove the sheet from the second partner and have them dance again, holding each other without the sheets between them. Freeze the sculpture and say, "What you saw before was *'falling in love;'* this is what we call *'rising in love,'* i.e., the ability to share your inside as well as your outside with your partner."

Real-life situation

Awareness and humor through teaching

"I was not meant to live in isolation."

The Fort

To explore an avenue of approach to the well-defended individual

M
Mechanics/Method

Invite the patient to explore manifestations of his co-dependency by honoring and identifying his defenses, representing them with pillows and using these to build a wall around himself. Therapist needs to be sensitive here and communicate to the patient that anyone would want to have protective walls from the pain he experienced when growing up. By empathizing with the patient, the therapist establishes trust with the patient, who knows that his defenses are honored.

With trust established, therapist can invite the patient to explore what it would be like to have a door and/or window in one of those walls so the patient could come in and out and others could, too.

The rest of this work would involve step-building, the patient connecting emotionally and perhaps using a "guardian angel" to explore what is outside the walls and to come back and report to the imprisoned patient.

Therapist's Note: This piece may be a good "shoehorn" piece to take the person into exploring, focusing and ultimately discharging his pain.

The guarded lifestyle of the individual

Learning, connectedness and validation for one's own process with awareness of its limitations, such as "things don't need to be this way anymore"

"I honor my defenses because they keep me safe. Today I choose not to be a prisoner of my defenses and I welcome doors and windows for my walls."

Four Concepts of God

Teaching sculpture to promote awareness that patients do have choice in their relationship with a God of their understanding

Select four individuals to stand and face group. Have first individual put his body in the shape that would best express Punishing. Have the next put his body in a shape that would best express Unapproachable. Have the third person put his body in a shape that would best express Conditional, and the fourth person put his body in a shape that would best express Unconditional.

Therapist then turns to the viewing group members and says that these represent the four styles of relationships. Therapist asks: (1) How many people would want a relationship with Punishing, a relationship that would kiss and punch you, one where you never knew when "the other shoe was going to drop"? (2) How many individuals would want a relationship with Unapproachable, a relationship with somebody who is not there? (3) How many of you would want a relationship with Conditional, a relationship that would require continued needless sacrifice and where there would never be enough of you? (4) How many individuals would want a relationship with Unconditional, a relationship that means, "There is nothing you can do to make me love you more or less, I just love you"?

Therapist closes with, "These are also the four concepts of relationship with God." One may choose which appeals to him most, and whatever the choice, it will be compatible with one's personal religion.

Relationship reality

Awareness and personalization of Higher Power

"I do have choices—I can have a God of my understanding."

118

Hand Masks

To explore how one "wears" his anger

Have the group members think of anger, and then use their hands to make expressive masks in front of their faces to represent what they do with anger.

Therapist's Note: Sometimes I've had the patient do this in front of a mirror. I then bring another group member behind the patient to be the expressive voice behind the mask as the patient observes his mask in the mirror. This can amplify the patient's feelings. I then ask the patient to drop "the mask" so his inside and outside can match by joining with the amplified voice behind him.

Defenses and avoidance of anger

Awareness of and permission to own anger

"I can survive my feelings."

Hot Potato

A teaching sculpture to illustrate how choosing recovery is actually an intervention on other family members

Have four group members stand in the middle of the floor, and toss one of them a pillow. The therapist says, "This is a hot potato. Every time you catch this pillow, you say 'ouch' and toss it to the next person." Soon after this starts, the therapist freezes the sculpture, removes one of the people from the quartet and says that one person has decided to stop playing the hot potato game.

Now start the sculpture up again. This continues until there is only one person left. Turn to the group and say, "When one person decides not to play the co-dependency game any more, he pulls out, and others have to handle the hot potatoes (i.e., dysfunction) more often. This means that people get closer and closer to owning their pain, feeling it more often and ultimately doing something about it."

Real-life situation and family recovery process

Awareness and understanding of the "ripple effect" of everyone's recovery

"The most loving gift I can give you is the truth."

Integration Sculpture

A teaching sculpture that shows the similarities between a multiple personality and an untreated co-dependent, as well as the need for integration in both

Set up one sculpture using the terms that one uses in working with multiple personality. Have "host" stand on a chair holding strings that lead to group members who are playing the "original personality," the "fragment personality," the "inner self-helper," the "alternate personality," and the "presenting personality."

Do some sharing about how these roles play a part in the workings of a multiple personality. For example: the host would be the executive and in control the greatest amount of time; the original would be the birth personality, the original state; the fragment personality (there may be more than one) would be limited to the expression of one particular part; the inner self-helper would be the serene, rational advisor part of an individual that could serve as a guide to the other parts of the multiple; the alternate personality would be the opposite of the original; and the presenting personality would be like the master of ceremonies (this is usually the personality that shows up for treatment).

Have all of these stand still, connected with strings (like spokes on a wheel) to the host (standing in the middle on a chair).

Now call "time out" and rename the parts to illustrate an untreated co-dependent. Rename the host—"the compulsions or co-existing dependencies", the original— "the inner-child"; the fragment—"unfocused or sideways anger"; the inner self-helper—"an angel" (who nurtured the core of the individual somewhere along the line); the alternate personality—"the manifestation of the disease process"; and the presenting personality—"the defense," which shows itself in treatment (e.g., a smile covering up pain, etc.).

Now explain that, just like working with a multiple personality, the elimination, modification and integration process is exactly the same as that which occurs when treating the co-dependent.

 Pathological process and process goal

 Awareness and understanding by emphasizing the importance of emotional recovery

"I am the sum total of my parts, and together I am whole."

Irrational Knot

A theme piece for group members to explore entanglement in and impact of co-dependency

Throw a long length of rope into middle of group and invite members (one at a time) to pick the rope up and twist, knotting it tightly while sharing a conflict that resulted from co-dependency. As an individual begins sharing, invite another group member to grab the rope and do the same. Keep this process going until all are twisting and tying the rope tightly and sharing aloud.

Freeze the sculpture and make group aware that this collective knot represents the interior of an untreated co-dependent and what such a person brings to all relationships.

Therapist's Note: Group processing is important after this piece; anger discharge may occur.

Co-dependency life events

Awareness, bonding and possible relief

"I've been the butterfly caught in the web of co-dependency."

Loving God With All Your Heart

To teach the difference between spiritualization (i.e., using God to deny reality) and spirituality

Select an individual to play Higher Power and place him on a chair. Select two others to represent a single person, with one playing the adult part of the person and the other playing the inner child part of the person.

Next, arrange these people so that they are holding hands. Put the inner child part of the person on the far left, the adult part of the person in the middle and the Higher Power on the far right. Have them hold hands, turn to the group and say, "This is loving God with all your head."

The idea here is that the connection with Higher Power, in this sculpture, is on an adult or cognitive basis only. Then move the inner child between the adult and the Higher Power, have them hold hands again, and turn to the group and say, "This is loving God with all your heart." Explain that the inner self (i.e., inner child) is our connection to our Higher Power and to all relationships.

Disabling self-worth

The importance and awareness of our emotions for our spiritual development

"Without my Higher Power, I am sentenced to a life of trying to put the square peg in a round hole."

Magic Mail

1. To reconnect group member with childhood losses
2. To exercise self-worth through forgiveness

Hand each group member a blank sheet of paper, invite them one at a time to stand and read a letter that they would like to have received when growing up. (Therapist should begin process with an example: "Dear Son, I am so sorry I was never there for you. I know now that I am an alcoholic. I am so proud that you are in recovery. Please forgive me for all the broken promises and pain that I know I have caused you. I could never express my love. This letter is long overdue. Please forgive me and know that in my heart I do love you very much. Love, Father.")

After each group member reads such a letter, have them tear the sheet of paper up and scatter the pieces on the floor. When last group member has read his letter, ritualize the closing with group holding hands and listening to music of emotional healing and forgiveness, such as "In My Life" or "You Needed Me."

This piece enables group members to realize that the person they have been holding resentment towards has been living inside them rent-free. When the group members begin to forgive others, they are actually forgiving themselves.

Therapist's Note: I like to leave the scattered pieces on the floor and do this piece as an opener for group work. I add this comment to the group: When we look at the pieces on the floor, it is hard to tell which ones are ours and which ones are someone else's. We all have a lot in common here. Let's recommit to the process and work above these pieces today." This motivates the energy towards healing.

Childhood abandonment and loss

Grief, validation of feelings, support, relief, resolution and ultimately forgiveness

"Expressing my feelings is always good news."

Magic Mirror

1. Group exercise to explore co-dependency patterns and their origins.
2. Illustrates patient's search for "missing parts"
3. Breaks down patient denial and provides bonding for the group

Have group members take turns tracing around their heads and shoulders on large sheets of paper with dark magic marker. When all have finished, have each patient tape his tracing up on the wall.

The group leader then announces that this will be a timeless look at each group member's emotional history. Then instruct the group to begin writing in their magic mirrors everything that they never liked about themselves, past and present. (It's always good to inject a humorous note at this point by saying to the group, "If there is anyone here who thought, 'Oh my gosh, I'll be writing until midnight!', the first thing you want to write in there is *perfectionist.*")

Examples of what the participants may write are critical, judgmental, low self-worth, alcoholic, etc. Regardless of whether a person is in recovery from alcoholism or not, if there was a time in his life that alcoholism was active, this could be written in the magic mirror. Other examples might be: my body is too big, my body is too wide, I smoke, I'm afraid of my feelings, I hate men, I'm cold to my children, etc.

Upon completion of this part, have the participants step back from their mirrors and select another color of magic marker. Have them go back to their magic mirrors, circle each and indicate off to the side whether that particular entry (e.g., judgmental) was more like mother, father or both. Some will circle more items than others, which is fine because there is no right or wrong here. Just ask the participants to do the best they can.

When they all are finished with this section, have them step back again and select another color. This time have them go back and circle (some will probably recircle) the parts more like their spouses, partners, husband #1, husband #2, etc. When the participants are finished with this part, have them sit down and invite them to share any insights, feelings or awareness that came to them as they were doing this exercise.

Therapist's Note: Through the processing, many feelings, particularly anger and grief, will surface at the close of this work. The advantage to doing this exercise early in the treatment week, or as an outpatient exercise, is to provide the therapist with data. It's also a way to "break the ice" with group. This exercise will help the group bond and encourage sharing. As most of this work is nonverbal, an additional advantage is that people will disclose their pain and issues in a non-threatening way.

 Historical self-defeating patterns

 The patient to own his issues; shows that he did not create this vicious cycle

"I am ready for new ways of living. Now all my past can serve my best interest."

T
Title/Technique

Patient–Therapist

 U
Uses

To confront professional denial

 M
Mechanics/Method

As this is a teaching sculpture, it may be good to do this early in a workshop or treatment week. Have one group member role-play as a therapist and another as a patient. Build denial between the therapist and the patient, using all of the "therapist's" unfinished business and invaders (e.g., family of origin, frozen feelings, attitudes, nicotine, affairs, alcoholism, chronic masturbation, etc.). Continue to build with props, role-playing, etc, and freeze the sculpture. Now have the "patient" start asking for help from the "therapist."

 S
Simulates

Real-life limitations

 S
Stimulates

Awareness of the need for therapists to be healthy

"Do I make my story someone else's story?"

The Pillow Family

Teaching sculpture to show transgenerational pathology

Have two group members (one male and one female) stand up, and have each hold one pillow, which represents their repression. Have them come together in an embrace, with pillows between them, and say that this represents marriage. Then say, "Now you have a child and, since what doesn't get worked out in one generation gets passed on to the next, this one-pillow family produces a one-pillow child."

Select a role-player for the child and say, "This child then grows up and starts building his adult dysfunction on a base of pathology, and so becomes a two-pillow person." (Give another pillow to this role-player). Because pathology seeks its own level, this person will marry a two-pillow person; (have him connect with a two-pillow person). Have these two people embrace and explain that this symbolizes marriage. They also raise a child (select another role-player).

This child gets two pillows because he has inherited this double pathology. This child grows up and is about to build an adult dysfunction on top of these two pillows. He becomes a three-pillow person and will connect with another three-pillow person.

Stop the sculpture at this point; explain that co-dependency is nothing more than "passing pain on to the kids." Close the piece with processing.

Therapist's Note: With this model, we can teach that things not only get worse but require even more medication than in previous generations.

The cascading effect of co-dependency

Awareness of the disease process and our society's need for an abundance of medicators

"Co-dependency is nothing more than passing pain on to the kids."

The Planet

Explores enduring patterns of perceiving, relating, thinking and feeling

Place large sheet of paper on the floor and draw as big a circle as possible. Introduce the circle as "the world" (i.e., the planet). Invite the patient to build a sculpture on top of the circle (using role-players, props, drawing, sound, etc.) that would represent his environment.

As piece progresses, engage the patient with the various parts of the sculpture. Patient may have to discharge feelings here and will certainly reveal his coping style and ways of interacting. Therapist can advise on how he can change and/or modify "the world."

Patient's style and view of reality

Awareness of needs, focus and choice (i.e., the bigger picture)

"It is my job to be my choicemaker. Choices expand my world and don't limit my vision to obstacles."

Separating Disease from Person/Parent

1. Allows positive feelings (if any) to surface
2. Separates a person from the disease
3. Promotes understanding and discernment
4. Allows discharge of feelings

Select a group member to role-play the parent and another to role-play the parent's disease (with devil mask, for example). As the participant addresses the "parent," have the disease appear and block communication to distract participant. (You may want to start with the "disease" sitting in a chair under a sheet, and the "parent" standing behind.)

At the crucial point in the process, remove the sheet to expose the "disease" to the participant. This creates valuable shock to energize the process. The "disease" will follow the "parent" wherever the "parent" will go. Allow piece to unfold.

Therapist's Note: One idea I've used here is that the disease is what we are angry at and the parent is what we grieve.

Living with disease

Fear, anger, grief, abandonment, abuse; focuses more properly on the disease than on the person

"I am not my disease."

The Statue

1. Animates and explores participant's dysfunctional family and relationships
2. Leads to new insights and perspectives on relationship toxicity
3. Helps people to experience the origin and impact of negative messages and expectations

Have the participant stand on a chair and sculpt himself in a way that he believes he is perceived by family and friends. Have participant freeze in that pose.

Next, have the participant's "relationships" (roles played by pre-selected group members) enter the room one by one and come up to the "statue." Have them walk around the "statue" and continue repeating their negative messages. The "statue" has no choice but to take it all in, loud and clear.

Powerlessness

Old frozen feelings for discharge

"I can evaluate my own behavior. Today I choose healthy messages that are accurate and up-to-date."

Tape The Child

1. To teach the distorting and disabling effects of co-dependency
2. To illustrate the recovery process

Have one participant role-play the co-dependent and have another role-play the disease of co-dependency.

With the co-dependent standing still, have the disease put a piece of masking tape gently over the co-dependent's mouth. Therapist will describe at this point how the "no-talk rule" begins in dysfunctional families.

Next, the disease puts one piece of tape gently over one eye of the co-dependent; therapist here explains how a co-dependent's reality begins to become distorted and results in seeing half-truth.

Then have the disease put a piece of tape over the other eye; therapist describes how the disease is now taking over completely so that reality is totally denied; repression is taking place.

Next, have the disease put a band of masking tape around the arms of the co-dependent, with the therapist stating that this represents the next stage of the process, where compulsion sets in and denies the individual choice.

Finally, have the disease put a piece of tape around the ankles and legs of the co-dependent, with the therapist stating that this symbolizes that the co-dependent isn't going anywhere; he is completely without choices and is now stuck in a "death-style." Now de-role the disease of co-dependency and have another group member come up and role-play recovery. Recovery first removes the tape from the patient's mouth, stating that this is the first step in recovery—we begin to talk about it. Then, as in the former process, remove the piece of tape from the first eye and say that people, when first in recovery, begin to see half-truth, stay confused, and tend to fluctuate back and forth between what is real and what is not real.

Have recovery then remove the piece of tape from over the other eye. The therapist then says that this represents when people begin to see a full reality. With support they can continue in their recovery and ask for help in breaking the bonds of compulsion. (Have recovery break the tape band around the co-dependent's arms and start to move his arms.

Then have the co-dependent bendover and break the last bond himself, representing that he has had help, had support, had therapy and now it is up to him to make the behavioral changes. Have that person then take one step forward to represent moving ahead with choices and behavioral change.

 The process of the disease of co-dependency

 Understanding, closeness within the group; sometimes produces sadness or hurt, and these feelings will need processing

"My understanding leads to feeling, my feelings to my healing, and my healing brings changes."

Transference Piece

Teaching sculpture to help patients understand experiential healing process and their own use of transference

Select individual to role-play "everyperson," and place four empty chairs behind him. Ask one group member to sit in each chair, and explain that the chairs represent the "safety warehouse" inside this particular person's brain.

Begin to build some of the messages in the "safety warehouse" by assigning one of the following messages to each chair: 1) the stove is hot 2) I don't like spiders and snakes 3) big people hurt me 4) anger is bad.

Invite the viewing group participants to share which messages are no longer accurate and up-to-date. Then, select another participant to stand up and represent a therapist. Have this "therapist" approach the "everyperson." At this point, have the four messages begin to talk. As the "therapist" talks to "everyperson," the messages in the "safety warehouse" drown out everything that the "therapist" says (e.g., therapist is saying, "Welcome to small group, I'm here to help you").

At this point stop the sculpture and ask the viewing group participants to share which messages need to be removed so that this person can feel safe and have healthy relationship choices. Of course, the two messages that will be kicked out are "anger is bad" and "big people hurt me." Now there are two empty chairs; this is where group leader can explain that once these messages are discharged, there is room for "the good stuff."

Bring two other group members up to represent positive messages such as "it's safe for me to express all the colors in my paint box" (feelings), and "I can make choices and protect myself"; place these people in the two empty chairs. It needs to be stated here that during treatment patients will be reacting to schedules, group members, roommates, authority figures, therapists, etc. and that this is a sign that the process is working. It also needs to be explained that there can be no successful treatment therapy without playing these old tapes - transference. This also provides the therapist with a reference point if any power struggles erupt during the therapeutic process, (e.g., "I want to call time out; this is a good example of what we were talking about at the beginning of the week. I would like to give John an opportunity to explore exactly what he is reacting to and what I represent to him").

Source of transference and projection

Participants owning their conflicts and understanding their own processes. Also provides permission for patients to look to themselves, knowing that something is coming up for healing and relief, and to encourage sharing of this material

"My past is no longer obscuring my present."

Truce

1. Invites the participants to take and share step 1 of the 12-step program
2. Identifies medicators

Make a white flag out of plain white cloth and a dowel stick. With the group in a circle, pass the flag around. When each participant receives the flag of surrender, have each share a medicator (addiction or behavioral compulsion) he has used.

Use the "step one" format (e.g., "I am powerless over nicotine and my life has become unmanageable). After the flag has made it around the circle, have the participants again take the flag and share three things their medicators have cost them.

Therapist's Note: A group discharge of anger towards the disease usually follows this piece.

The step one process

Honesty, openness and willingness to own personal medicators

"It is through surrender that I begin winning."

Relapse Sculpture

1. To provide awareness of the importance of a safety net
2. To demonstrate how to break the pattern of relapse

When a therapist is working with a chemically dependent person who is a chronic relapser, his co-dependency work needs to be validated, but the patient also needs to know that he has co-existent dependencies. It is important that the patient is aware that chemical dependency is a separate disease that requires a separate style of treatment, which works in tandem with his co-dependency recovery.

The therapist does this by asking the patient what is needed to stay sober one day at a time. As the patient begins listing tools such as AA sponsor, aftercare support group, prayer in the morning, etc., have group members come out and represent those tools. Then have a group member role-play the drug of choice and say "Action!" (It is prearranged that the "drug of choice" knows to go right over and grab the patient and say, "I've got you.")

Therapist then announces to the patient that he has just relapsed, and asks if there is anything else that needs to be included in his safety net. Patient may say, "I need some other tools", or "give me some help." Bring those people who are role-playing as tools up. (It's important that the tools understand that they don't do the work; they are simply tools.) This can be a stimulus to patients who are relapsing to gain insight into how they have been inter-acting with the tools of their own recovery.

The process continues with the drug of choice going to the patient and saying, "I've got you." Repeat this process over and over and start counting the relapses. The patient usually runs from the drug of choice, hides behind his tools, wants the tools to do the work for him, etc. Just let this process unfold. It usually takes about 5-6 relapses before the patient finds himself (sometimes with the help of the group) in the middle of the tools, closely packed in.

The idea here is that the patient needs to be surrounded with the tools in order to stay away from drugs or alcohol one day at a time. At the close of this piece, all the role-playing participants need to write their roles down on cards, and give them to the patient to take home.

Therapist's Note: This piece provides insight for all recovering people; processing of this work is usually important.

 Real-life situation and implementation of recovery program

 Awareness and identification of specific need for a safety net in one's personal recovery process

"I am responsible for my recovery. All my co-dependency treatment won't take root as long as I use chemicals."

Therapeutic Emotional Healing

Anger at Self

Discharge anger for the patient who believes that "it's all my fault, I'm the one who's bad, etc."

Have the patient lie on full-size sheet of paper on the floor; ask other group members to role-play the disease of co-dependency. Have them trace with dark marker around the patient's entire body, pausing every now and then to talk and make eye contact with the patient, saying things like, "I define your shape; I tell you what you'll do and how far you'll go, how you'll think about yourself, etc."

At the completion of the drawing, have the person role-playing as the disease stand at the far end of the piece, and have the patient stand up and look at the drawing. Remind the patient that he is extremely angry at himself and offer him an opportunity to get rid of the anger and get focused in a healthy way. Slide a pillow under the drawing, and hand the patient the bataka bat and encourage discharging on top of the drawing. As the discharge continues, the disease should continue to taunt and provoke the patient.

At some point, the therapist needs to freeze the sculpture and say that the patient is not angry at himself but at the disease.

The distorted thinking and disabling self-worth an individual carries in co-dependency

Relief and dissolves shame through rage reduction; builds awareness that the individual is not the disease

"I can separate myself from the disease, and discover a new me."

Anxiety Awareness

1. Demonstrates "stuckness," energy drain, avoidance and personal invaders of happiness
2. Shows difficulty in risk-taking and making decisions
3. Opens the door for additional emotional work

Place patient in corner, with one or two other group members holding him from behind and around the waist; this represents the power of the disease. Have the rest of the group in the opposite corner, representing patient's dreams (e.g., a relationship, girl of his dreams, the job he'd really like to have, the city he'd like to live in, children, etc.).

Have "disease" group members (with masks on) act like they are "casting the magic spell," and chant messages from the voice of the family-of-origin unconscious (e.g., "You will never have these" or, "Even if you had these things they would go away!" etc.).

As the patient's dreams and goals reach out to him with enticements, also have the patient try to reach for these goals and dreams. The voices of the family-of-origin unconscious chant at participant and try to block participant's vision.

A bleak, choiceless life

Anxiety, frustration, helplessness, anger. Heightens awareness of how one's power is drained away

"I will not be in bondage to or be intimidated by my disease, which denies me choice."

Bed and Curtain

1. Identifies invaders of relationship
2. Identifies entanglements
3. Claims inner child and sense of self
4. Identifies boundaries

Use pillows to make bed, and wall this off from patient's view by having two group members hold up a sheet. Add two group members to role-play spouse and parent of patient in the bed behind the curtain. Drop the sheet and animate the sculpture. Have the spouse and parent call out to the patient and pull him onto the bed. When anger builds, use discharge technique.

Emotional incest

Awareness, discharge, boundaries, bonding, assertiveness and individuation

"I am only responsible for my emotions. I retire from being my parent's parent."

The Big Head

For helping patients who "live in their heads" connect with their feelings

Have patient draw on a large sheet of paper an oversized head. Instruct him to write down current events and conflicts in his head.

Next, have somebody role-play the patient's inner child. Have him sit in a chair and have the other group members take the large head and stand behind the seated inner child so patient sees that this represents his thoughts and feelings.

Now, have the patient role-play a daily activity (e.g., going to work) and tell the patient to take his "big head" to work with him. Freeze the sculpture at this point and make the patient aware that he has just left his inner child (i.e., feelings) at home; this is how he is going to go into the world. Once this point has been made, take the "big head" back behind the inner child sitting in the chair and have the patient stand in front of "himself."

Therapist will ask the patient to respond on a feeling level to things he wrote down in the head. A question from the therapist might be, "How does your inner child feel about this, John?" Have "John" start sharing his feelings. Encounter bats and other props should be nearby and ready for the client to use.

The exaggeration of an individual's style and being cut off from one's self, resulting a "half-life"

Repressed feelings and awareness; opens the possibility of reconnecting and perhaps even rescuing the inner child

"I also need heart knowledge; otherwise I have direction but no choices."

Body Tracing

1. Identifies anger toward self
2. Identifies negative messages

 Therapist will need paper (large enough to trace around entire body) and marker.

Have participant lie face up on paper; trace around entire body, then have participant stand and look down at the outline. Instruct him to "fill in" the outline with negative messages and beliefs. (It may be helpful to have the other group members chant the messages as they are being written.)

Ask participant how he feels about himself. Use encounter bat for anger discharge. Be sure discharge is focused on the messages and beliefs, not on personhood.

Therapist's Note: The sculpture can expand to the point where participant's next piece would be where the messages come from.

 The negative impact of the disease

 Anger, relief, forgiveness and empowerment

"I am separating myself from the disease. The disease is familiar, but I am unfamiliar to me. I need a support system of people who will help me in this new welcomed relationship with the unfamiliar."

Build an Army

1. To discharge anger
2. To provide a sense of power and support (good piece for the "shut-down" patient)

With one group member role-playing the disease of co-dependency, invite the participating patient to create an army of support, with weapons, to attack the disease. The weapons are important, as the patient will instruct the soldier on how to use the weapon and what movement and sound effects it makes. Make sure the patient gives one soldier a "war cry."

When army is ready, have patient put soldiers in place around the disease, and have patient re-enact what each soldier is doing as piece unfolds. Patient will access feelings by animating and instructing his army.

At some point it may be helpful to have patient also show the disease what the army is doing to it, and to have the disease mirror the patient's expression of pain, hurt, fear, dying, etc.

Therapist's Note: Sometimes it is more effective to have a few group members volunteer to be soldiers for the patient and for them to have their own "weapons" already. Then teach the patient how to fight (have patient mirror the body and vocal expressions).

The energy needed to lance the emotional abscess and shows importance of doing the work yourself, for yourself

Repressed feelings of hurt, anger and safety

"I declare war on the disease as I make peace with my paint box."

Chase the Ghost Out

To help patient shed associations (i.e., with partner, friend or spouse) who are pressuring them to recover

After validating individual's feelings (e.g., patient may feel angry because spouse has gone through co-dependency treatment and has attached consequences to patient's getting treatment), have group member role-play the relationship with patient. With encounter bat and pillow, invite the patient to discharge the feelings he needs to express. With each hit of the encounter bat, have group member who is role-playing relationship back up a step until he is all the way out of the room.

Real-life choices

Validation of feelings, support, relief and self-acceptance, as the "ghost" gets separated from the patient's and group's process

"Am I in recovery for myself or someone else?"

Daymares

Explores childhood trauma

Invite the group members to scatter about the room and have them each think of a painful event of their childhood. Have them reenact this nightmare by role-playing all the people who were involved.

Therapist's Note: I have found that doing this non-verbally first, and then adding words and sounds, brings powerful results.

Painful events

New perspectives and release of stored pain; builds safer avenue for sharing

"Reality is my thoughts and feelings and not my past."

The Disease Imprint

1. For emotionally shut-down patients
2. For patients who are struggling with accessing their inner children
3. For patients in denial of their medicators

Validate the patient's defenses and invite him to "sit this one out" and take a look at the disease of co-dependency, so that he will know what his issues are and where he needs to go in recovery.

With the patient in a chair on one side of the room, build the patient's family-of-origin issues, inner child and repressed anger, etc. In the front line, put his major medicators (for example, workaholism, nicotine addiction, caretaking, etc.).

Now provide each role-player with a message; have them whisper this message all at once and continue to do so. For example, the inner child may be whispering, "I'm here, please come and get me," the workaholic may be whispering, "it's never enough, work harder," etc.

As the patient sitting on the far side of the room sees this sculpture in action, freeze the entire sculpture and ask this patient if his inner child can be heard. (You may have to start this piece again and then freeze it.) This will convey the important idea that with all "the noise" going on inside the patient, it's extremely hard, if not impossible, for him to "hear" feelings.

This may be all the therapist needs to do; however, be prepared to continue with this piece if the patient begins to respond emotionally. At this point, the goal would be for the patient to "turn the volume down" on the other distractions and associations that surround and drown out the voice of his inner child. The inner child may be rescued if patient wants to continue work.

The brain and life events of the patient and the patient's historical relationship with co-existing dependencies

 Mental photographing of patient's current state, and may also be a vehicle for discharge and finally claiming one's own power

"Am I looking at me or my disease?"

T
Title/Technique

Draw God

U
Uses

1. To explore unfinished business with one's Higher Power
2. To better understand one's current relationship with a Higher Power

M
Mechanics/Method

On a piece of paper, have patients draw a picture of the God of their understanding. When they are finished, have them draw themselves somewhere on that page. Therapist now may use the actual drawing to help produce expression of feelings in the patient, or build a sculpture from the drawing and involve the patient in that piece. Discharge of feelings will follow, and therapist should have proper tools, such as encounter bats and pillows, etc., to help facilitate conclusion of piece.

Therapist's Note: This may be worthwhile to do with entire group. It may also be important to bring in the sculpture of the "Four Concepts of God" to help integrate the reconnection of the patient and the God of his understanding.

S
Simulates

Old issues with God and/or church

S
Stimulates

Rage release regarding God and the church, healing, forgiveness, integration and reconnection

"It's okay for me to be angry at God—God can take it."

Fantasy Island

1. To explore relationships, dreams and wishes
2. To express feelings of loss
3. To confront one's reality

Give patient a magic wand of the kind that can be purchased in a toy store and have him build a dream family, or a picture of how he wishes life and relationships could be. Have patient direct the sculpture and provide role-players with movement and messages.

Repressed feelings will begin to surface; therapist should be prepared to "freeze" the sculpture, move the patient in and out of the roles, challenge the patient to confront himself and ask patient why this is not happening in his life right now.

Therapist's Note: This is a golden opportunity to provide patient with direction and step-building to make dreams come true.

Fantasy versus reality

Anxiety and direction to make the patient's goals in life obtainable

"Fantasy will kill you—reality never will."

Funeral

Provides vehicle for group members to release grief and express loss

With sheet and pillow, create "grave" in middle of room and invite group members to share a loss by writing the nature of the loss on a cardboard "tombstone." Grief is piggybacked until process is completed. Discharge of anger often occurs and encounter bats should be handy, as individuals will cry, "Why did you leave me?" etc.

Therapist's Note: This can be used for individual patient work as well. Anything is fair game in funeral therapy except the funeral and death of one's "inner child."

Childhood abandonment and loss

Grief and possible anger discharge

"When I deny my grief, I deny my life process."

T

The Mirror Dance

 U *Uses*

To provide a way for individuals to do their work and explore their pain nonverbally. (This is a particularly good piece for patients who tend to "live in their heads.")

 M *Mechanics/Method*

With the patient in the center floor, have group members come up to patient holding cards prewritten by therapist. These cards have on them the names of persons, places and things that are pertinent to the patient's process. As the patient faces each individual and reads the card that each is holding, the patient must begin to use his body to come up with a still sculpture that would best describe what is written on the card. The individual who is holding the card must mirror what the patient is doing (e.g., scratching his head, etc.)

The therapist should be prepared to have the patient interact with what is being mirrored in front of him at strategic points. One of the final cards might be "inner child"; this would bring closure to the piece. This sculpture opens up lots of possibilities, and it may be important to use some verbiage to assist the individual in releasing his repression.

Therapist's Note: It may also be important for the patient to create nonverbally other sculptures that would be in contrast to what is on the cards (perhaps more pleasing) as he completes the process with each mirror dance.

 S *Simulates*

The historical life events of pain

 S *Stimulates*

Repressed emotional pain by eliminating the cognitive part of the patient

"I can't change what I can't see."

Pain and Pleasure

To resolve conflicting motives

Invite patient to select a group member to role-play pain and another to role-play pleasure. Have patient address both, and then have patient stand in between and hold on to them.

Now bring other relationships into the sculpture and have pain and pleasure challenge and compete for attention (verbally and by tugging on patient) as the patient interacts with the sculpture.

Therapist's Note: Be prepared for anger release as patient confronts pain and pleasure and begins to see just what they are getting out of the relationship.

Internal struggle and self-defeating patterns

Anger, relief and clarity

"As I examine my motives in a place where it is safe to feel, I achieve resolution."

T
Title/Technique

The Perpetrator

 U
Uses

1. To provide vehicle for group discharge of emotions
2. To represent sexual abuse

 M
Mechanics/Method

Screen off half the room with a sheet by having two group members hold the sheet up. Have group members stand or sit on one side of the sheet and, on the other side of the sheet, have one group member wearing a gorilla mask and chewing on a teddy bear that represents the "inner child."

Therapist will talk to viewing group members before sheet is dropped and sculpture is exposed. Therapist says, "When the sheet is dropped, you are going to see something disturbing. Let yourself feel whatever it is you need to feel. I invite those of you who are willing to express those feelings to come up and do so."

The sheet is dropped and the group member (i.e., gorilla) on the other side is revealed (growling, chewing and abusing the "inner child").

The impact of the noise and movement when the sheet is dropped often sends a shock tremor through the group. It takes a few seconds for the viewing group to recover, and therapist should be prepared to guide them into discharge that is focused on abusers in their lives.

Therapist's Note: Rage discharge can be done verbally with towel and/or encounter bats and pillows, etc.

 S
Simulates

Real-life situations of abuse

 S
Stimulates

Repressed rage

"I can't go through my pain painlessly. Release brings joy."

Title/Technique ## *Piggybacking*

 Uses

1. Maximizes the energy produced by a work in progress
2. Way for group members to do additional discharge

 Mechanics/Method

Sometimes a powerful theme may dominate a particular group. During those times, set a sculpture idea up for a patient. As the theme emerges and the patient discharges (e.g., anger or grief), invite other group members to move in and do some of their work also.

Therapist's Note: I have found that this technique works well in draining the repressed venom (a little at a time) from the "rageaholic."

 Simulates

Behavior patterns

 Stimulates

Relief, bonding and group momentum

"When one person starts to heal, we all do."

Safety in Bed (Touch and Stop)

Provides patient with opportunity to internalize feeling safe and to experience control over his body.

Create a bed of pillows and invite participants to lie down in the middle of the bed. Surround the perimeter of the bed with other group members and refer to them as guardian angels. (It is important that the participant not be touched during this exercise.)

As the participant lies down, ask him to take a mental photograph of the surrounding people; then have participant close his eyes and, with some soft music playing in the background, have the participant just experience what it is like to feel safe and protected in his own bed.

It may be important to have some of the group members whisper messages of assurance (e.g., "I'm still here" or "I won't go away" or "Nobody is going to hurt you today"). The participant may begin to have strong feelings, particularly sadness and grief, as he experiences the protection of the guardian angels.

As piece continues, invite the participant to select one person other than the group leader with whom he feels safe and invite that person onto the bed.

As this is done, ask the participant in the bed to ask the selected person if he will love the participant. As this is done, the selected person agrees. Then invite the participant to challenge himself and ask the selected angel to love a part of the participant's body. This could be a finger, cheek, forehead, etc. As the selected angel agrees, have that nurturing begin with a caring touch, and have participant close his eyes and take this in.

As the piece progresses, have the participant ask the angel to stop. As the angel stops and moves away, remark to the participant that this is what a loving person would do. A loving person will stop when you ask him to.

Then invite the participant to continue this exercise by asking the angel to start and stop at his own choosing and by memorizing what this feels like. As piece comes to a close, remark to participant on the bed that he has experienced control over his body with a loving person, and also that his body is no one else's but his own.

 A protective environment

 Empowerment, nurturing, safety, calming and the awareness that one can be close and still have boundaries

"When I take risks I learn what is right for me. I grow in self-worth and learn to trust myself."

The Secret Circle

1. Gives participants opportunity to leave excess baggage and gain relief
2. Provides vehicle for additional discharge work

Have participants sit in a circle with pillows leaning on their backs. With their eyes closed, have them think of one secret burden they'd like to leave behind.

Therapist then goes around the circle taps a person on the back and asks what he would like to leave. The participant shares, and tries to pull the burden (pillow) off his back. (Therapist holds one end of the pillow so the participant has to work to pull it off; all the while the participant continues to repeat the secret.)

The pillow finally gets placed in the center of the circle. The therapist then asks participant what the cost of this secret burden has been and gives him the encounter bat to discharge on to the burden (pillow in circle). This gets repeated until all clients dump a burden and beat it into the circle.

Therapist's Note: Some insightful processing can develop as the pillows are stacked in the center of the circle and group members are obscured from one another!

Excess emotional baggage

Forgiveness, relief, discharge of anger

"Today is the day I take care of unfinished business."

Shut-Down Participant

1. Wakes up the participant's repressed emotions
2. Explores the self-defeating messages and their origins
3. Breaks down denial

Have the participant sit on the floor and ask him for feelings. Whatever the participant says, have a group member wear a dark mask (Lone Ranger type) and sit in front of the participant, repeating what the participant says in second person (e.g., if participant says, "I feel nothing," the masked person says, "You feel nothing"). As long as the participant feels nothing, have the masked person say things like, "Good, thank you for listening to me. You are a good boy as long as you don't feel."

Sometimes the participant will start feeling his repression in his stomach, chest, etc. If so, have the masked voice push a pillow on that spot on the participant's body and say things like, "You must listen to me!" and "You will not feel that!" The masked person should sound spooky and evil and his hands should move as if "casting a spell." Participant should be made aware that there can be no forward progress with his work unless the voice is confronted and discharged away.

Repressed emotions

Anger, awareness

"My life urges are stronger than my death urges."

Signs and Symptoms

To provide the patient with a way to challenge his defenses

Have patient sit surrounded by group members who are role-playing verbal and nonverbal observed signs (e.g., heavy sighing, tight jaw, etc.) and complaints (symptoms) that the patient has shared; for example, "I feel numb" or "I'll never change." Patient needs to know that these defenses are honored but also that they need to be challenged. It may be important to move the patient out of the center of the circle and have somebody role-play his inner child by having the inner child sit in the center of the circle as these manifestations of co-dependency surround it. The goal is for the patient to challenge these defenses as members of a group or individually.

Therapist's Note: If a patient balks by using a particular defense such as shaking his head, heavy sighing, breaking eye contact, putting hands in pockets, etc., it may be important to feature this in a sculpture down the road so that the sculpture will continue to unfold and not be shut down. In this way, the defenses are working for the individual as opposed to against his healing process.

Distorted thinking, distorted feeling and disabling self-worth.

Awareness and repressed feelings

"This disease is not my fault, but I am responsible for my recovery, and part of my recovery is learning to ask for help."

Stealing From Self

To illustrate self-abuse, loss of self and loss of personal power

After tracing the body of patient on full-size sheet of paper, have him stand in front of the outline and begin sharing his needs with the people he is in conflict with. The patient must cut a piece of "himself" out (tear with hands or use children's round-edged scissors) and hand it through the tracing to the role-playing person standing on the other side. (Hands can also come through the holes and grab at the patient.)

Therapist's Note: I have used this piece to work with diagnosed kleptomaniacs and have included the items they've shoplifted on the other side of the body tracing. After patient has cut enough of himself out and handed it through to the item or person on the other side, anger was released around the theme of "you owe me!"

Relationship complications

Awareness and releases anger and grief

"Living in balance means always keeping enough for myself."

Step Through The Window

 Allows participant to step into his fears and challenge them

 Have two group members hold a rope high between them. Explain to the participant that this rope represents a window; the side he stands on represents the familiar. When he steps through the window, he will be standing in the unknown.

Invite the patient to step through the window and face his fears. Use other group members to role-play the fears -this can be used as a theme piece for entire group.

Therapist's Note: As the fears are addressed, invite the patient to challenge the fears with anger, as they are keeping him from getting on with life.

 The unfamiliar

 Motivation and awareness; promotes self-worth through risk-taking

"Are my fears engineering my personality, or do I have my own blueprints?"

The Totem

1. Introduces how co-dependency affected the entire group
2. Discharges anger

Select one person to stand on chair and represent the disease of co-dependency. Now invite the group to "dress" the disease (e.g., put props on the disease and in the disease's hands; have group members put the disease in a pose and give it movement and messages to say).

As this piece unfolds, invite group members to write down on separate sheets of paper something the disease has cost them and to tape these sheets on the disease. Encourage group members to share these losses aloud with the disease. (At this point discharge of anger and grief will surface; have encounter bats and pillows, etc., handy.)

Therapist's Note: A good way to close this work is with group affirmation chant of, "I am not the disease."

The life events and complications of co-dependency

Openness, closeness and connectedness of group, discharge of anger and grief, and provides relief

"I admit that I have, but I no longer worship, the disease."

T
Title/Technique

Trampoline

U
Uses

For patients who have trouble retaining their feelings

M
Mechanics/Method

Explore with patient ways that he historically has over-reacted to positive and negative feelings and ways that these feelings have "bounced" out of his system.

Once this connection has been made, invite the patient to reenact these scenarious and to imagine that he is on a trampoline and jumping up and down as he shares. Therapist needs to go up and down with the patient as he is going through this process. As feelings begin to surface, therapist needs to join hands with patient and show support and understanding.

S
Simulates

Exaggerated style of connecting emotionally

S
Stimulates

Awareness that patients can survive their feelings and heal emotionally as they begin to "catch" themselves going into their hysteria

"I can surrender to the experience of the moment because I can survive my feelings."

Tunnel of Love/Tunnel of Rage

To help augment a sculpture already in progress or to be used as a piece in itself

Have group members stand in two lines facing each other. Have the "star" of the sculpture walk slowly down the middle; it is sometimes helpful to have the "star" proceed with his eyes closed and hands touching the group members as he goes to keep his balance and stay connected.

The group members in the line repeat messages that are caustic, hostile, etc., and/or simply growl angrily in a growing crescendo as the "star" gets further down the row. Once "star" is at the end of the row, there is an opportunity to do more focused emotional work. Once that work is completed, have "star" turn around, and have group members join hands to form an arch and create the "tunnel of love." The "star" proceeds slowly along the "tunnel of love." As each group member is passed, affirmations of love and support are given to the "star."

Original life-threatening trauma, validation and nurturing

A flood of feelings. Every feeling from rage to joy is possible.

"My journey has purpose—always."

Vicious Cycle/Mad Machine

1. To access feelings
2. To provide patient with view of self-defeating lifestyle

Build sculpture by using group members to role-play parents and inner child.

Give the parents a rope to represent reins that are attached to the inner child in front of them. This "chariot" should be augmented with negative messages like those the inner child received growing up (e.g., one parent may be saying, "Work harder" and the other parent may be saying, "Please your mother").

In front of this arrangement, have group members who represent promises, goals or other "carrots in front of the horse." One group member is also in charge of seeing that the inner child receives medication for his pain.

At a given signal, activate the sculpture. The viewing patient begins to see how his inner child is carrying excess baggage from childhood through life in pursuit of unachievable goals. As the inner child strains at the reins of his parents and reaches for the "carrot in front of the horse," freeze the sculpture. Have a group member who represents a goal slide a medicator such as food, nicotine, relationship, etc. in front of the inner child. Have "goal" say "Nice try, have some of this, it will make you feel better, try again later," etc.

As piece proceeds, participant will be given opportunity to address each of these parts of sculpture. Therapist should be prepared to freeze and dissect the machine at the appropriate times.

Powerlessness over addiction and need for medication

Frozen feelings and awareness

"Insanity is doing the same thing over and over again and expecting different results."

Wailing Wall

1. Group discharge piece
2. Vehicle for additional data-gathering

There are two ways to proceed here. (1) Have patients draw pictures of their pain and anger. (2) Use sentence completions. When using sentence completion, verbalize the sentence stem; have the patients write it and finish the sentences on their own. The sentence stems I like to use are:

> I am different because. . .
> The color that best describes me is. . .
> My most negative thought of myself is. . .
> My three greatest fears are. . .
> The earliest memory of my mother is. . .
> The message my mother gave me is. . .
> The earliest memory of my father is. . .
> The message my father gave me is. . .

When the drawing of sentence stems is completed, have patients tape their pages on the wall. Instruct them to face the wall and push against it firmly with their hands. (They should step back a little bit from the wall so they can begin to apply some firm resistance.)

Have the group members look at the drawings or the sentence completions and have them say aloud the message that is speaking most strongly to them at that moment. Have them repeat that sentence over and over again. The entire room will be whispering a message all at once.

The therapist then operates as a "football coach" and challenges the group to get louder and louder and to push harder and harder. The resistance against the wall will bring up powerful feelings that are repressed.

Distorted thinking and feeling

Old frozen feelings for discharge and the need for updating self-appraisal

"My tremendous power has many voices, and they all are singing my song."

Walking in the Rain

Provides vehicle for sharing loss and experiencing grief

Cut and tape strips of paper approximately 4 inches wide and 8 feet long and give one to each group member. Instruct each person to write his losses of the past on the paper. When they are finished, have the group members tape one end of the long strip to the ceiling near center of room.

Next, explain to the group that the hanging strips are our tears; invite members one at a time to step into "the rain" and shed their grief with the group. Having outside group members repeat in wispers what the sharing participant says while in "the rain" augments the process.

Personal history

Repressed feelings and relief

"I've been crying on the inside for years. Now it is time to cry on the outside."

War Zone

1. Resolution of unfinished business
2. Access to feelings
3. End the war within self

Create obstacles, "booby traps," negative messages and fear (use props and role-players). Have the participant crawl through the "jungle" and try to find safety. Have a grave with the "inner child" partially in it, and have the participant try to rescue the child and get out of the "war zone." (Participant will have to challenge the war in order to escape and save the child.)

Original life-threatening trauma and events around loss

Sense of importance of survival; "victory", i.e., the war's over; and restoration of motivation to the "inner-child"

"I am a survivor; my injuries are no longer a big deal. They are now little deals because I can do something about them."

You're Jerking Me Around

Group participation in discharge and sharing

Have group members sit in a circle. Therapist tosses into the center of the circle a medium-to-large-size teddy bear representing the "inner child." Have all group members grab hold of this teddy bear. Instruct group members to concentrate on the hands that are holding their "inner child."

With concentration on the hands, challenge the group members, all at once, to verbally release feelings by repeating the names of all the people who have a "piece of their kid." While this is going on, have the group pull and tug so that the tension and resistance are created to help amplify and release repression.

Entanglement and loss of self

Discharge of anger, provides relief and leads to further group bonding

"If you don't respect my boundaries, you don't respect me."

Self-Worth, Child Within, Higher Power, Humor

 The Adult World

 To explore, through the eyes of a child, what being an adult means

 Have patient sit on floor and invite him to direct a sculpture that will depict what the "adult world" looks like through the eyes of a child. This piece usually starts out being "fun," then leads to sharing frozen feelings and childhood memories that are painful. It is a good idea to process this piece with the group upon completion.

 Behavior learned in childhood

 Clarity, childhood identification, memories and feelings

"I didn't get much when I was growing up. The adults in my life had little, if anything, to give. This is a fact, not blame."

Borrow a Mother and Father

Provides nurturing to patient

Have patient select a "healthy" mother and father; invite patient to bring them to life by giving them dialogue and movement, and by having them support an interest or hobby the patient may have or have had, etc.

As the patient becomes more involved with the piece, let patient have a moment when he gets to hear and experience something he was denied as a child. To close this piece, have the patient introduce his "mother and father" to the group and share what he likes about each.

Childhood losses

Grief and relief as historical pain is explored

"It is never too late to have a happy childhood."

Build an Adult

1. To create clarity and direction for patients who have trouble retaining their inner children
2. To help patient recognize needs

Ask the patient to verbalize the qualities that a loving parent would have (e.g., being responsible, protective, consistent, fun, encouraging, etc.). As the patient proceeds, have the group members role-play these different qualities and arrange them in a tight grouping in front of the patient. (It's helpful to have a scribe write down on note cards what each of these qualities are and tape the note card on the selected role-player.)

There are usually six to twelve parental qualities verbalized, and the therapist may find it necessary to help engage the patient in modifying these qualities as there may be some overlap. Once this process is finalized, the patient is validated for knowing what is required of a loving parent.

The therapist then reminds the patient that given this understanding, it is now his responsibility to seek out ways to help develop those qualities in his life. The cards can be collected at this point and given to the patient to serve as a reminder as to where they need to direct their energies in aftercare.

Therapist's Note: Sometimes I've found it helpful to build the adult and bring in someone to role-play co-dependency. The disease stands in front of the patient to stimulate anger toward co-dependency and to empower the commitment for the patient to recover. So this, as with all the other sculptures, is open to variety.

I have also used this as a group piece so that everyone, collectively, builds an adult for themselves and has an understanding as to what they need and where the direction of their recovery needs to go.

The missing pieces of the patient's parenting and childhood

Opportunity for patients to parent themselves and to begin getting their needs met

"Learning to love yourself is the greatest love of all."

Coat of False Color

To examine misplaced identity

Hold a sheet up and say that this represents a coat we have worn to hide our true selves. Invite the group members to wrap the sheet around themselves one at a time and identify and role-play the sheet as a person, place or thing they have used to lose themselves in and what losing themselves gave them. (For example, "I am work, and because of my job I am important" or, "I am my 25-year-old daughter - she gives me a reason to exist.")

Once a person has shared, that person removes the sheet and passes it on to the next group member; repeat until all have shared. When this is over have group members face a mirror (one at a time) and affirm themselves the exact same way—only without the coat and role-play. (For example, "I am important" or "I no longer live for anyone else.") Process work when all have affirmed themselves.

Fantasy self

Awareness of self-worth

"I am here to rebuild my security."

Compare and Contrast

1. Dissolves emotional distance (especially good for "the lost child")
2. Inaugurates self-discovery

Select a half-dozen group members to role-play a patient's characteristics that are similar to and opposite those of his parents. Animate the role-players as needed, and place them in two lines with the similar and opposite characteristics facing one another. The patient moves down this row and explores his historical relationships with each characteristic represented.

Identity (past and present)

Merging with real self, separation from parents (i.e., not self) and affirmation

"I used to believe something was always wrong. Now I believe something is always right."

Demolition Derby

1. To have participant experience the impact of negative messages
2. To provide a stepping stone to the origin of those negative messages

Have group members get behind chairs so participant can't see them. (Have a pillow on each chair.) Next, have participant write down his negative messages on cards and tape the cards on the chairs. The group members behind the chairs chant the negative messages and push the chairs ahead of themselves, following the participant wherever he goes.

Finally, have one of the group member role-play an important relationship to the participant. Have that person stand at the opposite end of the room, and have the participant walk toward that person and try to have an intimate relationship. The participant will be blocked by the pursuing chairs (whose holders are chanting the negative messages).

Therapist's Note: Have the encounter bat handy, as participants will want to challenge those messages (thus affirming themselves).

Invasiveness of our negative messages

Self-worth, relief, frustration, anger, awareness and power

"I have a choice in what I import and export."

Emotional Reconstructive Surgery

1. Closes open emotional wounds
2. Builds self-worth and trust
3. Affirms participant's resources

Therapist will need to have available: index cards, ball of string or yarn, tape, markers and soft music.

Have the participant lie face up on the floor (it is more comfortable with pillows). Play soft, relaxing music. As the participant closes eyes and relaxes, group members write loving affirmations on cards. One at a time they whisper the affirmations in the participant's ear and gently tape the cards to the participant's abdomen (or wherever his pain is).

When all have done this, the group gathers around on the floor and tosses a ball of yarn back and forth. Each thrower holds on to a piece of the yarn after it is thrown, so the ball is unwound further each time. Have the participant open eyes so he can see the "network of love" above. Then tuck in the string around the participant, "sewing the love in."

Patient's need for support and affirmation of self

Positive feelings, self-love, nurturing, safety, trust, risk-taking and healing of emotional pain

"I don't short-change myself. My process is special to me and I respect it as well as the time it takes to heal."

The Gauntlet

1. Explores/exposes abusive patterns
2. Provides a way to move participants to the sources of their pain
3. Lets them reclaim the "inner child."

Have group members stand in line (one behind the other) facing the participant. Each group member is role-playing a relationship (e.g., former lovers, former spouses, current lover, current spouse, etc.). At the end of the line are the participant's parent or parents. This lineup can be in descending chronological order, i.e., the most recent relationships are at the beginning of the line. Halloween-type masks can be worn to add to the tense atmosphere.

The first role-player holds the participant's "inner-child" (teddy bear or doll). As the participant discharges feelings towards each role, that role-player moves aside but passes the "inner child" back to the next role-player. Continue until the participant is faced with family members at the end. When participant discharges feelings here, he can retrieve the "inner child." Encounter bat and pillows should always be between the participant and the role-players.

Serial dysfunction

Discharge of anger, grief, provides relief; promotes self-worth and healing

"I don't have to pay for friendships. My 'inner child' alerts me to what is love and what is abuse."

Gender Piece

To eliminate gender transferences in group and to promote emotional healing of the sexes

Draw a large stick figure of a man on a long sheet of paper. Next draw a large stick figure of a woman on another long sheet of paper. Tape the drawings opposite each other on the wall; have the males in the group surround the stick figure of the woman and the females surround the stick figure of the man.

Introduce this sculpture by talking a bit about "pollution" in general terms as well as pollution of the person. Add the idea that these polluted messages are inherited. State with emphasis that *we did not make these messages up* and challenge the group members to take this opportunity to get this pollution out of their systems.

Give each participant a marker and instruct them to write on the drawing every negative message, word or phrase that they know about the stick figure in front of them. As the individuals write, have them announce aloud what they are writing. This quickly becomes quite a shouting match; on occasion, discharge of anger will be necessary, so encounter bats and pillows should be handy.

As the group finishes writing these messages, have them, without speaking or touching, switch sides. Have the women take the drawing of the woman down from the wall and stand behind it, and have the men take the drawing of the stick figure of the man off the wall and stand behind it.

The two groups should now be facing each other, standing behind their drawings so they can see the labeling and messages put on their gender. The therapist then challenges the group by saying, "If you are tired of reacting to the 'wrapping paper' and missing the gift inside, at the count of three, I want you to tear the paper, step forward and hug the person or persons in front of you." Group leader then counts to three, the paper is torn, and as the two gender groups embrace, deep healing takes place.

Therapist's Note: It is useful to have a tape of a thunderstorm as the messages are written throughout this piece to add to the climate for discharge. Lower the volume of the tape slowly at the end and announce that "the storm is passing." Close the piece with the sense of commitment to gender peace or start an affirmation chant.

 The impact of our inherited negative messages

 Awareness, power, equality, self-worth, anger, frustration, relief, honesty

"I have male parts and I have female parts. I honor all my humanness."

Me and My Shadow

1. Explores the disease
2. Explores the self
3. Challenges and makes peace with the past

Turn the lights off in the room and have group members stand in a line with their backs to the therapist. Therapist then turns flashlight on and begins to move the beam so the group members' shadows are cast on the wall they face.

Introduce the shadows as the co-dependency past and have the group members share aloud their relationships with co-dependency. As each member shares, instruct him to move towards his shadow until group members are flush with the wall (and their shadows). Discharge of feelings may be in order here, and pushing against the wall would help bring it up.

When this part is complete the therapist states that "our co-dependency creates our own obstacles; if you are ready to commit to having your shadow fall behind you instead of leading the way, turn now and move slowly towards the light." At this point group members turn and begin to walk towards the therapist holding the flashlight.

Have them form a tight circle and move into an affirmation chant.

The personalities of the disease and the turning point in one's recovery

Commitment to recover, bonding, relief and surrender

"My past is part of my recovery base. As long as I keep my eyes towards the light, my shadows stay behind."

Negative Bus Station

1. To expose and explore self-defeating messages
2. To introduce healing through humor and play

Have group members write ten negative messages about themselves. Set up a bus station (two rows of chairs). One at a time, have participants enter the station and carry on a creative conversation with each other using their negative messages, e.g., "I hope the bus comes soon, but then again, nothing good ever happens to me," or, "I'd like to ask you for a date, but I'm not good enough." At some point, the group usually explodes in laughter. The "Affirmation Chant" would be a great second piece to close with.

Therapist's Note: Therapist should stand by to direct and give cues in the beginning. It usually doesn't take long for the group to take over and do without the written script.

Negative impact of self-defeating mesages

Laughter, healing, awareness, bonding

"When I change my messages, it helps change my beliefs. When I change my beliefs, it helps change my behavior. When my behavior changes, I have choice."

Rescue of Inner Child

1. Gives access to feelings
2. Relieves emotional suppression
3. Introduces inner-child relationship
4. Allows discharge of feelings
5. Good tool for the "frozen" patient

Build a family sculpture, and have the participant select a group member to play the "inner child."

As the child gets "buried" by the family dysfunction, have the child call out, "Why won't you help me?" If the participant still remains frozen, have a rope attached to participant and the "inner child." As the "child" cries out, have the "child" pull on the rope. If the participant does not react, have a group member (playing the disease) hold the participant from behind, and command "stay still," "don't move," etc.

Abandonment

Participant owning conflict, integrates the child with the participant, releases anger, transfers worth of the child to the adult

"Am I motivated to recover or resigned to repeat?"

Self-Portrait

1. To get patient to engage in his own inner processes
2. To get patient to own where he is in the disease process

Have patient describe himself with three nouns and three verbs. Then have people representing these nouns and verbs stand in front of the patient; have him put them into a pose that would best describe that noun or verb.

The therapist will then direct the piece, as the interacting people begin to have a dialogue. Discharge may occur with the parts that the patient doesn't like. The idea here is that the patient can indeed repaint his portrait.

Contemporary mirroring of self

Frozen feelings, relief and renewed sense of identity and self-worth

"Is my portrait priceless, or am I still painting it?"

Talk With God

To provide individual and/or group members an opportunity to share their losses with a God of their understanding. (This may be used as a piece in itself or in tandem with the work already in process.

Have a group member stand on chair; wrap sheet around this individual and announce to the group that this person represents Higher Power.

Invite the group or participant to go up to "God," make contact, and share a loss with Him. (If this involves the loss of a loved one, e.g., an unborn child, death of sibling, spouse, etc, have participant ask "God" to give him an opportunity to say good-bye and to have closure with this relationship.)

Then invite the participant, when he feels ready, to ask this "God" to watch over and protect this relationship loss. This is a good opportunity for continued grief work in group. Therapist should be prepared to use "piggybacking" in order to get full effectiveness out of this sculpture.

Therapist's Note: Frequently during this sculpture, the group member role-playing "God" cries. It is important to have participant look into the eyes of "God" and for the therapist to comment: "See, God has feelings, too. God is sad that you suffer so."

It is also important during the piece to have "God" impart to the patient that it is important to forgive himself, with the knowledge that no matter what he did, he was "a little kid trying to be safe," and "now, with recovery, you can be responsible for your actions."

I usually like to use a female to play "God." This does several things; most importantly, it gives the group members an expanded awareness of what a "God of your understanding" can mean, and it provides another frame of reference for any chauvinistic attitude about a Higher Power.

The need for forgiveness and relationship with Higher Power

Expression of repressed emotional grief and self-forgiveness

"My spirit can't soar until I cut my chains."

Under the Basket

To work with patient's adult shame, state of isolation and style of avoidance

Have patient sit on floor; have remaining group members stand and hold sheet over top of patient so the patient appears to be "under a basket." Since the patient on the floor cannot see the faces above, but can only hear inter-action going on, this may in itself serve to heighten the awareness of feelings needed for this person to proceed in his work. Standing group members may also ask each other if they would like to "play," and then engage not only in dialogue, but perhaps in singing as well. At this point, therapist should be on the floor with the patient, engaging in dialogue and in taking an emotional temperature check. Time-out may be called by therapist for the patient on the floor to experience the "dead silence of isolation." (There are lots of opportunities for the work to unfold.) The goal, however, should be for the individual to challenge himself and "break out" of this confinement. As this happens, a towel is a good vehicle to use to discharge the repressed feelings. The patient on the floor will twist and pull on the towel as the feelings surface.

Therapist's Note: Whatever the vehicle of discharge, it's always important to "animate" the insides of an individual so that the work is not purely physical. This can be done by a sound, scream or actual verbiage. It may also be helpful at some point to have the standing group members drop the sheet on top of the individual sitting on the floor. The therapist explains that this represents a "cloak of shame," and challenges the sitting participant to reduce the shame with anger, using the sheet as a tool as described above.

Repressions, co-dependency life events

Freedom from shame through rage reduction; also stimulates cravings and urge for relationships

"I no longer require my relationship with aloneness. I deserve to be full of life."

Closures

Affirmation Cards

To give group members ways to share some gifts they have received during the day's process

Hand each group member a note card, and have them write down one gift that they received from the group process that day. After they have done this, have them share what they wrote with the group.

Now provide the group members with this insight: ask how many people have heard the expression, "If you see something negative in somebody, you see it in yourself." Usually more than half have. Now tell them the opposite, which is, "When you see something positive in somebody, it's because you . . . what?" Individuals, invariably, are astonished to find out that it's because "I have that quality in myself."

Now have them claim this affirmation for themselves (e.g., "Today in myself I saw . . ."). Group members are now replacing negative beliefs and messages with up-to-date, accurate, affirming, positive statements.

Therapist's Note: Sometimes, at the end of the treatment day, I like to have individuals write down something positive that they saw in themselves. I ask them to share only one of those attributes, so they learn to always "keep enough for themselves" and "don't give it all away."

A safe learning environment

Feelings of self-worth, understanding and closeness with group

"If I don't tell myself who I am, someone else will; and I may not like what I hear."

The Altar

To allow group members to do an additional piece of discharge work (good closing piece at the end of intensive treatment week)

Place a cardboard box against the wall, and one-by-one have group members come up and place props and/or losses written down on note cards on this "altar." The "altar" gets covered with props and events that were important for the group members' processes.

Invite the individuals to come up one last time and kneel before the altar (which represents co-dependency—the worship of false idols in the form of people, places and things). During this time, ask the individual if there is anything else he needs to say or get rid of at this altar. Have encounter bats and pillows handy, as individuals may want to discharge some final piece.

Therapist's Note: It's often good at the close of this exercise to lead the group in affirmation chants such as "I am not the disease."

Inventory and review

Sense of closure, additional discharge of anger and/or other residues of repression

"Am I in charge of my life or am I taking charge?"

Nap Therapy

1. To relax and wind group process down
2. To put spacer in between blocks of sculpture work

Invite group members to lie on the floor and listen to soft music while therapist reads them a story. Therapist needs to impart the idea that this may be challenging for some individuals, but that part of recovery involves calling "time-out." Therapist reads story and group members relax. When story is completed, therapist should wait and have group members internalize the peace that they are experiencing at the moment; then ask them to share their emotional temperatures.

Safety and childhood need for and right to nurturance

Feelings of safety, nurturing, appreciation and unconditional love

"It is perfectly appropriate to take a vacation from self-improvement."

Paper Doll

1. To visualize and share goals
2. To integrate recovery

Place assorted colors of construction paper on the floor. Invite group members to select one color and tear it into a shape that would best describe how they would like to be some day. (For example, the results may include a star, circle, a whole person, etc., but leave this open and allow their imaginations to take over.) At the completion of this step, invite the participants to share the shapes and explain their significance.

Recovery goals and realistic expectations

The playfulness of recovery, sharing and self-worth

"My dreams come true because they are now a rhythmical part of my creative being."

Quality of Life Workshops

Over the years, we have found that we can help most people who come to our programs. There are many levels of help, and there are many reasons people come to us.

We often hear that there are many ways to help people; the problem is, how do you get people to seek help? To try to address that problem, I put together a series of workshops that serve as "community intervention." These workshops are offered at a low fee to anyone interested. The workshops are designed to:

- provide information
- awaken feelings
- confront reality
- offer hope

The workshops have two important goals:

1. To bring immediate help and direction to those who are able to use the information and implement some positive changes in their lives.

2. To intervene with those who need ongoing care and to help them accept this need and seek the necessary further care.

Our experience in this program is that it has been a stepping-stone for many. These workshops can be offered by:

- private clinicians
- treatment centers
- churches
- community agencies
- community education classes, etc.

We will share with you the topics we cover in our programs and a sample flyer that goes into the community. You will need to write your own content for the workshop. If you need further help with the content, you might want to consider attending an Onsite Training Institute workshop and getting some further ideas. There are 10 sessions all together.

Course One has six sessions:

1. **The Family Trap:** A painful family system affects everyone in it. Learn the ways addiction or other preoccupations trap every family member in difficult survival roles. Learn what co-dependency is and why it affects everyone in a preoccupied family.

   Family Trap video is shown in this session.

2. **Family Communication:** A crucial step in breaking out of the family trap is learning to communicate. Acquire tools to help you begin talking about family problems as a start towards solving them.

   This session uses sculpture and exercises to improve communication.

3. **Healing Unfinished Business:** Learn how unresolved issues from the past affect your life in the present. Find out what you can do to work through and get rid of old pain so you can live more fully and freely in the here and now.

4. **Intimacy and Resentments:** With an emphasis on forgiveness of yourself and others, this session will help you learn how to resolve old issues and deal with resentments that keep you from fully enjoying intimate relationships.

5. **Another Chance:** A painful childhood and family history don't have to be forever. Learn how family treatment can give everyone another chance for healing and recovery.

   Another Chance video is shown.

6. **I'm The Only Me I've Got:** Realize your own potential to be a whole person, living fully as a physical, spiritual and emotional being. Learn ways to develop self-esteem and enhance your own self-image.

   In this session, each participant does a collage, and people go home with a sense of renewed self-worth.

Course Two has four sessions:

1. **Choices: Big Deals and Little Deals:** What do we really want? What choices can help us move out of the places we feel stuck? Learn to identify the "big deals" and "little deals" in your life around families, jobs, friends, work and play.

2. **Intimacy and Boundaries:** When is it safe to open up and be vulnerable? This day focuses on ways to maintain healthy boundaries at the same time you take risks to nurture intimate relationships.

3. **Spirituality and Emotional Healing:** Moving toward a lifestyle of fulfillment and serenity includes developing one's own individual spirituality. Use tools such as meditation, affirmations and a self-image collage to help clarify your own definition of spirituality.

4. **Creative Living:** Learn to use all the colors in your personal paint box! Use music, art and humor to become more aware of your own creative potential and to develop your creative power. Celebrate your growing self-worth.

Use, add, delete! We hope this community intervention will be as good for you as it has been for us.

Bibliography

BOOKS BY SHARON WEGSCHEIDER-CRUSE

All materials are available from Nurturing Networks, 2820 West Main Street, Rapid City, South Dakota 57702.

Another Chance: Hope and Health for Alcoholic Families, Second Edition
  Science and Behavior Books
  P.O. Box 60519, Palo Alto, CA 94306

Choicemaking
  Health Communications, Enterprise Center
  3201 SW 15th Street, Deerfield Beach, FL 33442

Learning to Love Yourself: Finding Your Self-Worth.
  Health Communicatons, Enterprise Center
  3201 SW 15th Street, Deerfield Beach, FL 33442

Coupleship
  Health Communications, Enterprise Center
  3201 SW 15th Street, Deerfield Beach, FL 33442

Understanding Me
  Health Communications, Enterprise Center
  3201 SW 15th Street, Deerfield Beach, FL 33442

The Miracle of Recovery
> Health Communications, Enterprise Center
> 3201 SW 15th Street, Deerfield Beach, FL 33442

BOOK BY JOSEPH R. CRUSE, M.D.

Painful Affairs: Looking for Love through Addiction and Co-Dependency
> Health Communications, Enterprise Center
> 3201 SW 15th Street, Deerfield, Beach, FL 33442

BOOK BY SHARON WEGSCHEIDER-CRUSE AND JOSEPH R. CRUSE, M.D.

Understanding Co-Dependency
> Health Communications, Enterprise Center
> 3201 SW 15th Street, Deerfield Beach, FL 33442

VIDEOS BY SHARON WEGSCHEIDER-CRUSE

The Family Trap
Another Chance

OTHER BOOKS

[The remaining books are not available from Onsite.]

Alcoholics Anonymous. *Twelve Steps & Twelve Traditions.* New York, 1953.

American Psychiatric Association. *Textbook of Psychiatry.* Washington, DC: American Psychiatric Association Press, 1988.

Ashton, Heather. *Brain Systems.* New York: Oxford University Press, 1987.

Bergland, Richard. *Fabric of the Mind.* New York: Viking/Penguin, 1985.

Branden, Nathaniel. *The Disowned Self.* New York: Bantam, 1971.

Brilliant, Ashleigh. *I Have Abandoned the Search for Truth, and Am Now Looking for a Good Fantasy.* Santa Barbara, CA: Woodbridge Press, 1980.

Cousins, Norman. *Anatomy of an Illness.* New York: Norton, 1979.

Engel, Jorgen; et al. *Brain Reward Systems and Abuse.* New York: Raven Press, 1987.

Franklin, Jon. *Molecules of the Mind.* New York: Dell, 1987.

Gold, Mark. *The Good News About Depression.* New York: Villard Books, 1987.

Kopp, Sheldon. *If You Meet Buddha on the Road, Kill Him.* Palo Alto, CA: Science and Behavior Books, 1972.

Perls, Frederick S. *Gestalt Therapy Verbatim.* Provo, UT: Real People Press, 1969.

The Psychotherapy Handbook. New York: New American Library/ Meridian, 1980.

Satir, Virginia; and Baldwin, Michele. *Satir Step by Step.* Palo Alto, CA: Science and Behavior Books, 1983.

Stevens, Barry. *Don't Push the River.* Provo, UT: Real People Press, 1970.

Index

About the Authors

Sharon Wegscheider Cruse is the president of Onsite Training and Consulting, Inc. in Rapid City, South Dakota. She received the Marty Mann Award for "Top Communicator in 1982 in the Field of Alcoholism." In 1985 she was the founding chairperson for the National Association of Children of Alcoholics. She chaired the country's first national conference on adult children (1985) and the first two national conferences on co-dependency (1989-90). Also the consulting editor for *Focus* magazine, her work includes many books, numerous videotapes, and two films on how alcoholism affects families. Often featured on top radio and television shows and in popular magazines, she is in demand as a speaker and has conducted workshops throughout North America and in Europe, Central America, Australia, and New Zealand.

Joseph R. Cruse, M.D., is the medical director of Onsite. A certified addictionologist, he was the founding medical director of the Betty Ford Center and a clinical assistant professor at the University of South Dakota School of Medicine. Having authored and co-authored many books, he has also made many appearances on national television and radio shows.

George Bougher, M.Ed., is the clinical director of Onsite and has extensive training in experiential therapy. An accomplished and experienced therapist, he is an artist whose creative skills enhance his clinical work.